# SAVING
# SARAH

# SAVING SARAH

## Janet Murnaghan

ST. MARTIN'S PRESS ❧ NEW YORK

SAVING SARAH. Copyright © 2018 by Janet Murnaghan. All rights reserved. Printed in the United States of America. For information, address St. Martin's Press, 175 Fifth Avenue, New York, N.Y. 10010.

www.stmartins.com

Designed by Steven Seighman

The Library of Congress Cataloging-in-Publication Data is available upon request.

ISBN 978-1-250-13528-5 (hardcover)
ISBN 978-1-250-13529-2 (ebook)

Our books may be purchased in bulk for promotional, educational, or business use. Please contact your local bookseller or the Macmillan Corporate and Premium Sales Department at 1-800-221-7945, extension 5442, or by email at MacmillanSpecialMarkets@macmillan.com.

First Edition: September 2018

10  9  8  7  6  5  4  3  2  1

*To the bravest, fiercest, most determined person I know:*
*Sarah. You inspire me every day!*

# SAVING SARAH

# 1. The Truth

The machines whoosh in a loud, rhythmic pattern as they force air in and out of my baby's crippled little lungs. Sarah looks tiny and fragile under the fluorescent lights of the hospital room. She is ten years old but only weighs about fifty pounds and stands the height of a seven-year-old. Her growth has been severely stunted by her long, painful battle with cystic fibrosis (CF)—a battle to breathe.

I try to speak, and she struggles to hear me. Sarah has been waiting for a double lung transplant for eighteen months. During that long wait, she has lost more than the pieces of her childhood—her ability to hear has been stripped away, too. The same medication that has kept her death at bay has taken her hearing bit by bit.

I shout so she can hear me over the loud, pulsating machines. "Sarah, should we hang all your photos on the door, or do you want some closer to the bed?"

Her sweet face, voice, and little smile are engulfed in a mask that encircles her nose and mouth so completely that it is hard to even hear her speak. "Mommy, I want some of them closer to the bed this time."

Sarah and I are both trying to focus on decorating her new room instead of on our fear.

"Okay, hon, what about the paper lanterns you made? Should we hang them from the ceiling here, too?" I am smiling.

"Yes, Mommy, I love them."

Sarah and I have a tradition each night as we lie awake in her hospital bed trying to go to sleep; we pretend we are in Hawaii instead of at Children's Hospital of Philadelphia (CHOP). We run the air-conditioning on high, and the air gently rocks the paper lanterns on her ceiling like an ocean breeze. We then turn on her Twilight Turtle, which is a baby nursery toy. It creates a blue ripple of waves across the ceiling and plays a sweet song. We lie there and talk about our Hawaiian vacation. Neither of us has been to Hawaii, and we are certainly not there now, but we pretend as she drifts off to sleep. Now we hang the lanterns in her new room as we prepare for yet another night of waiting, hoping, and fearing what will happen next.

While I am the cheerleader, the questioner, the emotional one, Fran is steady, dependable, and quiet. He does not wear his emotions on his sleeve like I do, but don't let that fool you—he is breaking to pieces on the inside. Today, Fran is focused on our move from 8-South to the pediatric intensive care unit (PICU). He has taken dozens of trips from one floor to the other. When you have lived in the hospital for three months, changing rooms is like moving a child home from college.

Over the last ten years, Fran and I have created a comfortable rhythm for managing life and family while Sarah's in the hospital. Since her diagnosis at one, she's been inpatient several times a year for a couple of weeks at a time, every single year. Our family has two modes, "normal" and "hospital" mode. Typically, we are like any other family, our kids have multiple activities and playdates—life's busy. We shuffle all the usual hubbub of family life around Sarah's medical needs, which include hours of chest physical therapy and multiple medications. We make it work, putting the kids' needs first, Fran and I taking whatever is left over—which, incidentally, is not much. When Sarah's in the hospital, we divide and conquer, which usually means for one, maybe two weeks, Fran handles life at home with our other three kids, while I manage Sarah's care in the hospital. It gives the kids stability, everyone knows what to expect, but it's not a very marriage-centered approach. Fran and I live very separate lives during these admissions. I don't micromanage him, and he doesn't micromanage me. I could not care less during "hospital" mode if the kids at home eat healthfully or their clothes match. Is their hair combed? I don't know and frankly don't care. When Sarah's in the hospital, I let it go; that's his job, he's a great dad, and I don't get involved. Similarly, I handle most decisions at the hospital alone. Before now, it's really worked, but this time around's been harder, longer. I feel lonely and like I am carrying the weight of the world on my shoulders alone here in the hospital. Sarah's never been this sick before.

We fill this PICU room—our new "home"—with pictures and hang colorful decorations to make it feel homier. Sarah's bed is draped with pink stuffed pigs, and the walls are adorned with her favorite posters from the *Twilight* movie series.

Sarah's new room is dark and dim; it sits on the interior of the hospital, so there is no natural light at all, just a view of the hospital's atrium. It is depressing.

When you move to a new floor in the hospital, it's like being readmitted. A flood of doctors and nurses come in and out asking endless questions. But it is Sarah's team I care about—the lung transplant team. They have stood by her since she was listed for transplant almost eighteen months ago. They are professional and kind, but mostly I love them because I can tell that they, too, care about Sarah and are heartbroken to be watching her slip away as we lose this battle. You can see that it's personal for them. So, when one of Sarah's transplant doctors enters the room, we are eager to talk to him.

Fran and I are desperate for even a glimmer of hope or good news. We dig for it in our questions, though the answers have been getting gloomier and gloomier. This doctor, James Kreindler, MD, is a particularly pessimistic guy. Dr. Kreindler is a smart man, good at his job, and so caring and sweet with Sarah, but in all situations, he will always be sure to tell me the worst-case scenario. I guess if I were facing reality at this moment, I would say he is a realist. Our reality sucks, and he is brutally honest about that. Perhaps I call him pessimistic to shield myself.

At this point, most of our conversations about Sarah do not happen in front of her, so the three of us step out into the hall. I can feel my hands start to sweat and shake. There is a white-hot knot in my stomach, and we begin today's round of questioning.

My voice trembles as I try to speak. "Well, the one good thing, at least, is that her lung allocation score [LAS] is increasing, so even though we are in the intensive care unit, we are getting closer to 'the call,'" I say nervously, trying to add my silver lining to our situation while suppressing the tears.

Dr. Kreindler's brow wrinkles with a confused expression, and I think, *Oh, geez, here it comes.*

He looks at me quizzically. "What do you mean?"

"She is sicker. All her blood work looks worse. So, her LAS score will reflect that," I say defensively.

"But Sarah's LAS score doesn't matter because she's under twelve," he declares.

In my mind, I am screaming, *What?* But I try to muster something more intelligent and articulate than that. "Well, I know her LAS does not matter for pediatric lungs, but she is listed for adult lungs now, too, and it matters for adult lungs," I say emphatically.

"No, it doesn't matter for adult lungs either since she is under twelve," he says. He is infuriating me. Why, in this moment, is he trying to take away my last hope? And he is wrong. I am certain of it. I refuse to believe him. I want to scream, "Stop saying this to me. Stop! You are wrong, so, so wrong!" Instead, I say, "What are you talking about?"

I can feel my eyes stinging with the burning of the tears I am trying to hold back. I know I am right. For weeks, months even, I have made sure that with each worsening in her lung function and blood work, Sarah's LAS has increased accordingly; I have borderline harassed her nurse practitioner, Katie Oshrine, ARNP, about it.

"Sarah is under twelve. She is on the under-twelve list, which means it is primarily time accrued," he explains. "When she lists for adult lungs, she only receives them after all adults in the region, regardless of LAS, turn them down first."

"Then why would she have an LAS at all?" I ask, annoyed and knowing in my heart that Dr. Kreindler is as wrong as can be.

"Everyone has an LAS. All kids under twelve do. It's just meaningless," he explains.

*Oh, this man.* Why can't he let me have this one thing? I am about to burst into tears, and I don't want to do it in the hallway in front of everyone. So, I end the conversation and return quickly to Sarah's hospital room. I try to swipe the tears from my eyes and put Dr. Kreindler's words to the back of my mind. I decide that I will email Sarah's nurse practitioner and get to the bottom of things. In the meantime, I must return to "mommy mode." There is nothing worse for Sarah emotionally than seeing me upset; it sets her on edge.

Our room is a surprisingly upbeat place, filled with cheerful activity. Despite the dire situation, we are constantly playing games, doing crafts, and watching movies. Sarah loves to sing; she even makes up her own songs and talks about being onstage someday. She wants to be famous, as a lot of ten-year-old girls do. She has a sweet, young nature about her, very innocent in most ways, but at the same time, she is wise way beyond her years. Sarah is all too aware of the seriousness of her situation even though Fran and I have tried to shield her from it. She is like her mom, happy to put it in the back of her mind, locked away tight.

Tonight, it is me, Fran, and my sister Sharon playing another rousing game of Monopoly. Monopoly is Sarah's favorite game and a nightly request. She has her own figurine, a little metal three-legged pig, as her character. It was a gift from her cousin Maggie, and it holds special meaning for her. The first reason is because it's a pig, and anyone who knows Sarah knows she loves pigs. Second, it is a three-legged pig, and though you would expect it to fall, it doesn't—it remains standing. It feels symbolic of Sarah and her will to overcome CF. She has asked that I tape this pig to her hand when she goes into the operating room for her new lungs.

Sarah requires each player to take an oath on beginning the game. You must raise your right hand and say, "I do solemnly swear to stay and finish this game of Monopoly until its completion." We never complete a game, but everyone in the room knows that we will continue until Sarah falls asleep. This usually happens past midnight. Tonight, it is sooner, which is good. I am emotionally exhausted and overwhelmed. It has been a full day with a lot of heartache.

## Fran (Daddy)

Moving. Fun adventure, right? We have been living in the hospital for about three months now, and we have collected more "stuff" than we ever have on any trip to the hospital before. Of course, we have never lived here for so long. My job is to take this entire room of memories that Sarah has collected and rebuild it in the new room that we will be moving to.

So, I look around and survey all the stuff we have been collecting for what seems like a lifetime now—the clothes, toys, coffeemaker, wine. As I am contemplating it all, a woman comes in with a red wagon and a few plastic bags. She tells me that if I need more bags, I can get them at the front desk.

I am fine with my job, as it allows me to occupy my mind with something other than the obvious reason we are moving from our comfortable 8-South pulmonary floor to the PICU. On 8-South, Sarah has friends and a whole community, which is great for her. The nurses here are like family, and we have known many of them for years. Her CF friends are inpatient often, and although they can't be together physically, they can often be found sitting in the doorways of their rooms, gaming on a device.

For me, 8-South has allowed me to fall into a strange and completely unrealistic state of mind, where I believe Sarah eventually will get her lung transplant. It is easy on 8-South to think that Sarah isn't *that* sick. If she were, we would be somewhere like the PICU. And now we are moving there. I am fully aware that this is not a good move. I pack up the room and take a dozen or so trips down a few floors with my moving wagon. We settle in and start a fresh game of Monopoly.

Just hours before Sarah's move to the PICU, I had my sisters, Lora and Sharon, bring all the kids in to see Sarah. The doctors told us this morning that the day we have been dreading had finally arrived—Sarah needed to move to the PICU because the risk she will crash and need to be intubated is now high. We knew this might be the last chance for her brothers and sister and her cousins to see Sarah for a long time.

Fran and I have three other kids—Sarah's two brothers, Sean and Finn, and her sister, Ella.

Sean is in first grade and just turned seven. He is an exceptionally gifted child academically, and he is sensitive and emotional. I am trying to manage him from afar—unsuccessfully, I might add. Sean is a mama's boy, and the separation of the past three months has been more than he can handle. He is pretty much falling apart. The guilt of not being who he needs me to be right now weighs heavily on my heart. I feel I am failing him. Sean is starting to understand the seriousness of the situation. Although we have had many other hospital stays, we have never been away from home this long.

Finn is four years old and in preschool. He has gone from having a full-time, stay-at-home mom his whole life to being in school full-time. He is very easygoing and unfazed by all the changes, at least on the surface. My sister Sharon's four-year-old and five-year-old boys are his best friends, so he is loving the "extended sleepover" at her house. Finn does not "get" the implications of Sarah's illness; he is just too young to understand.

Our daughter Ella is a special situation. She is eight. We adopted Ella from Ghana; she came home just seven months ago. She is sweet, kind, and gentle. She has experienced tremendous loss in her life, so it is easy for her to imagine the worst-case scenario. When I told her that Sarah and Mommy needed to move into the hospital until Sarah got new lungs, she tearfully asked, "Is Sarah going to die?"

"No," I replied emphatically.

"Are you going to send me back to the orphanage?"

Horrified that she would think this, I replied, "Never, ever, baby. You will stay at home with Daddy, and when he can't be there, you will live with Aunt Sharon and with your brothers and cousins until Sarah is all better."

She told me courageously that this was OK with her. "I can do that."

Sharon tells me Ella spends a lot of time bustling around her house, trying to be helpful while Sharon pushes her to just be a child.

My heart is bursting that I can't be the mommy they all need right now. I am so homesick for my children, my family, my life. It's a triage approach; Sarah needs me the most right now, so that's where I stay, but it's heartbreaking. I do not spend any time questioning this decision—I'm very decisive—but I mourn the loss of everything.

Their visit earlier today was emotionally exhausting in many ways. They came into Sarah's hospital room one by one at first so they could each have a moment alone with her. They each have what we call "lovies": special stuffed animals they cherish and sleep with every night. Once a kid picks a lovie, we buy duplicates in case we lose this special friend. Invariably, though, they end up wanting all their lovies with them every night.

Today, they each decided to bring one of their lovies to give to Sarah. They believe their lovies will protect her and comfort her. It was so sweet, beautiful, and heartbreaking all at the same time. One by one, they hugged Sarah, snuggled, talked, and gave her their lovies. The magnitude of this gift was not lost on her. This was the giving of a child's most prized possession.

After Sarah's siblings, each of her cousins came in. First, my sister Sharon's kids who are young like mine—Robby, nine; Jayden, seven; Sawyer, five; and Alex, four—came in. Sweetly, they also had decided to give up their lovies. Sharon's kids are like siblings to mine and vice versa. We live right next door to each other, and before Sarah's downward plunge, I was nanny to Sharon's kids. When they left the room, Sarah had a bed lined with special stuffed animals.

Next, my sister Lora's kids came in. They are in high school and have always doted on all their little cousins. Gina, eighteen; Maggie, seventeen; and Brian, fifteen, fully grasp that Sarah's condition is very serious. They had brave faces on and led the "littles" in a party for Sarah. Sarah's older cousins are mentors to her. They have had a special bond with her from the moment she was born and have always showered her with attention. This morning at Sarah's party, they led all the kids in singing "You Are My Sunshine" to Sarah. This is Sarah's song. We began singing it to her when she was just a newborn and later as a comfort for her when she got sick.

Sarah has been planning for transplant for a long time. It has been an anxious wait, and rather than worry about the giant medical obstacles ahead, we have been preparing a party for the day she gets the call that her new lungs have arrived. She has bought "blinky balls"—the type you would find at Fourth of July fireworks events. When we found out this morning that the odds are that Sarah will be intubated and sedated within days (and not awake if we ever get donor lungs), I encouraged her to do the party today (a "pre-transplant party"). We assured her we would buy more supplies for the day she gets the call. "It's so special that everyone can come today. Let's have a party now, too." And so, we threw Sarah the best PICU send-off party we could muster.

### Sarah

I am upset and scared to move to the PICU, or as I call it, "the scary floor." I love 8-South! My nurses, therapists, and child-life specialists dote on me and treat me like their friend; they play board games with me, and we have even created a "wall of fame" for the winners of all the games we have played. The door leading to my bathroom is filled with sticker cards for all the games we have played. I feel safe here. On the scary floor, I know no one. When I move, I have to say good-bye to all my 8-South friends. I cry and beg Mommy to get them to let me stay.

Pa is here. He's Mommy's dad and my best friend. I can be myself with Pa. I don't need to pretend to be strong or brave. I love Pa. He comes every day to sit, play, and snuggle with me. He acts like nothing is different or wrong at all. Even before I moved into the hospital, when I was sick and on oxygen and I couldn't run and play like other kids, Pa would come every day and support me. Today, he is there when I learn I have to move away, when all of my fear comes out.

Mom, Dad, and I decide to invite my sibs and cousins to the hospital for a party. I love seeing my siblings and cousins, who are basically siblings, too, because we are so close, but I feel like I need to be brave for them. My stomach hurts all the time. I haven't eaten in a long time. I get all my food through IVs, and I retch and retch all the time. The pain in my stomach is the worst part right now. It's harder than oxygen and the machines. I just can't get comfortable anymore.

So, I try very hard not to show my pain, to be brave for all the other kids. I am the oldest of the younger bunch, and I know they are scared. It's important to me not to frighten them. The celebration is exactly what I need. I am brave for them throughout the whole thing, and this makes me feel proud. I don't want them to be scared. To me, this is a celebration of what's to come. I know once I get to the scary floor, I will get my lungs soon. The lungs will be ready once we get to the scary floor.

# 2. Sarah Is Dying

Fran and I sit next to Sarah's hospital bed feeling hopeless. The machines whir around us. Sarah sleeps heavily, undisturbed when nurses and doctors come in making their rounds, listening to her chest and shifting her body. It has been a few days since I showered, and I'm still in my jammies—the kind you buy in the hospital gift shop—because that's where I shop now. Fran is slouched over in the chair he slept in all night. He looks like he hasn't shaved in days. We are no longer dividing and conquering. Fran and I are both at the hospital full-time now. We don't speak. Last night's conversation with Sarah's doctor weighs heavily on us. Dread fills my stomach. We have an all-hands meeting scheduled with the transplant team this morning.

Samuel Goldfarb, MD, is a pediatric pulmonologist and medical director of the lung transplant program at CHOP. Dr. Goldfarb is Sarah's primary transplant physician and our ally. He is kind, caring, and laid-back and has an extremely positive disposition. Dr. Goldfarb's positive outlook suits me. Fran and I joke that he is the rainbows and sunshine to Dr. Kreindler's gloom and doom. And while they do have very different dispositions, they are both exemplary doctors, and we are blessed to have them in Sarah's corner fighting with us. Since Sarah's admission more than three months ago, they have seen her every day, seven days a week, without fail.

The team arrives and leads us into a narrow side room that looks like the type of room you might cram a bunch of residents into. It is lined with computers, leftover coffee mugs, and backpacks. Its bright white paint and loud lights are a startling contrast to the dark, dim hospital room we have just exited. The room is clearly not meant for this arrangement.

"So, I heard about your conversation with Dr. Kreindler last night regarding Sarah's place on the twelve-and-over list. Unfortunately, he's right," Dr. Goldfarb explains apologetically.

I am floored, speechless.

"Because Sarah is ten, she is on the under-twelve list, which is primarily time accrued. As you know, Sarah has been at the top of that list for over a year now. She's really competing with herself. It's just a tough list with very few offers," he explains.

"When we placed Sarah on the twelve-and-over list, we hoped to open up her donor pool, but her odds on that list aren't very good. Any available lungs will be offered to all older candidates before they will ever be offered to Sarah. I'm sorry. I wish I had better news."

Unlike last night, I don't argue; I know it's the truth. Silence fills the room.

"Sarah doesn't have much time left," he explains compassionately. "We are going to need to make some hard decisions in the coming days, and we thought we should talk about those things now while we are not in a crisis."

"Okay," I mumble. Fran is quiet, too. What can we say?

"We are watching Sarah carefully," he continues. "Ideally, we want to intubate her before she crashes on her own and we are in an emergency. But once we intubate her, the clock is ticking. We will have two weeks, maybe. So, we want to be careful not to do it too soon or too late.

"There's another alternative we would like you to consider," he explains. "It's called *ambulatory ECMO*. It's relatively new in lung transplant medicine. We would have a bypass machine take over the work of her lungs, and rather than keep her sedated, we would wake her and expect her to exercise."

We do not know anything about ECMO, which stands for *extra-corporeal membrane oxygenation*. It is hard to even know what to ask. The thought of Sarah awake on bypass and exercising is terrifying. Alongside us is a member of the pediatric palliative care team. They are my emotional partners and my voice when mine fails me. Their job is to ask the hard questions, to help us get all the ugly facts. As I sit in silence, they begin to ask questions.

"If Sarah never gets a transplant, what will her death look like intubated and sedated, versus on ambulatory ECMO?"

*What will her death look like?* I am not prepared for this conversation; this is not OK. She is ten. She is a baby. *Her death?*

"If she is intubated and sedated, she won't feel a thing," explains Dr. Goldfarb. "If she is on ambulatory ECMO, she will be awake," he says gently.

"Why would we choose ECMO, then?" My mind is spinning as I ask this question.

"Because it may provide her extra time to wait for lungs. And the exercise will help her body be stronger physically when she goes into the operating room."

"How many times have you done ambulatory ECMO on a waiting lung transplant patient?" Fran quizzes.

"Once," says Dr. Goldfarb.

"How did it end?" I ask, fear ripping through my voice.

"The patient did not make it to transplant and died from complications of the ECMO after a long wait."

"Oh my God! No way!" I say. "We cannot continue to torture

her over and over." I'm panicking. I know there is no one in this room to be upset with. They have been nothing but supportive, fighting for my daughter, never giving up on her, but my emotions are just pouring out of me. How did it ever come to this?

"Give it some thought," Dr. Goldfarb says gently.

I gulp down vomit as tears sting my eyes. The torture Sarah has endured is too much for any adult, but for a ten-year-old child, it's unthinkable.

### Fran

Once we settle into the PICU, many of our interactions with doctors turn to how we will manage the end of Sarah's life. Now, straight up, they are doing everything possible to secure lungs for Sarah, as they are for all their patients needing organs. The reality is that under the rules, we don't have much of a chance.

We also start to meet a more extended team. It is not a good sign of the direction you are going when the medical team begins to expand. We meet a cardiologist. We have never needed cardiology before. We meet the ECMO team and are asked to consider some terrifying scenarios. They all mean well, and they save people's lives every day, but it is terrifying.

I am very careful to pay attention and ask questions.

This is not the first time I have watched helplessly as someone I loved fought courageously and endured pain in the hope of a medical miracle. My mom, Regina, died ten years ago of cancer just one month before Sarah's birth. She was only fifty-nine years old. Her cancer had been advanced (stage four) by the time it was discovered, but she fought until the bitter end. She accepted the torture of surgeries and chemotherapy because she wanted to live for us—her family. And I believed up until the very end that she would defy the odds and make it despite the grim diagnosis. She didn't, and I lost my best friend.

For a long time after my mom's death, it was almost impossible to think of anything but the suffering she endured. At times, it was hard to remember her before the hell of cancer. I don't want that for Sarah, but I'm also not ready to give up. I'm terrified of losing Sarah and afraid my fear will guide my decisions—leading to a horrible end. I'm afraid I will fight when I should be letting her go peacefully.

When I pray, I don't pray for a miracle; I pray for strength and wisdom. I commonly recite the Serenity Prayer: "God, grant me the serenity to accept the things I cannot change, the courage to change the things I can, and the wisdom to know the difference."

I beg God, *Please, please stop me when enough is enough. I need to know when to stop. Please tell me when to stop.*

As I leave this meeting feeling defeated, I'm not sure what the next steps should be. These are enormous choices with terrible implications. How do I decide all of this for her? Do I owe her a choice? When Sarah was diagnosed with CF at one, we chose Howard Panitch, MD, attending pulmonologist, director of the clinical programs, and director of the technology dependence center for CHOP, to be her attending physician. From then up until she was listed for a lung transplant, he managed all her care.

Over the past year, we have gently transitioned to the transplant team, but that has never stopped Dr. Panitch from staying involved. He comes to Sarah's hospital room regularly for social visits, and I know he stays connected medically, too. Sarah loves him, and so do I. He is one of our most trusted confidants at CHOP.

After one of his recent visits with Sarah, he pulled me aside. "Sarah knows she's dying," he said.

"No, I don't think so," I said. "We've been very careful to shield her," I explained.

"She said good-bye to me today, thanked me for everything I've done for her. It wasn't our usual 'see you next time' conversation. She thinks she's dying," he explained.

I was shocked.

"I tried to reassure her, saying, 'Hey, I'll see you in a couple of days, this isn't good-bye.' But she knows," he said.

Knowing this, and knowing the suffering she faces, Fran and I make the painful decision to include her. We have tried so hard to shield Sarah. We have screened her view of the pain we know is on the horizon. But we can't climb this mountain for her. We need to give her a choice, even if we don't want to. We need to shatter the innocence we have worked so hard to preserve, if it's even still there. But how do you talk to a ten-year-old about her possible death? Fran and I agree we must give Sarah the choice of whether to continue fighting.

I sit in bed with Sarah and begin painfully. "Sarah, Mommy and Daddy want to talk to you about something serious," I say carefully.

"OK," she responds sweetly.

"You have been so strong and so brave over the past couple of months. We are so proud of you! The doctors are coming up with a plan to help you fight until your lung transplant. But it's going to get a lot harder. You are going to get a lot sicker." My voice quivers as I continue.

"Some of the things the doctors want to try will be very hard," I say. "If this is too much . . . If you can't do it anymore . . . If we are asking too much of you—you don't have to keep fighting. We will stop all of this if you want to stop fighting."

"Stop fighting and do what?" Sarah questions, wide-eyed.

"Stop fighting and . . . prepare to go to heaven," I say gently.

"Stop fighting and die?" she shouts. "Mommy, I will never give up, ever, so don't you give up on me! Promise me, Mommy, that you will not give up on me!" Tears are streaming down her little face. She looks so fragile and weak, yet so fierce.

"Sarah, I will never give up on you," I say emphatically. "Daddy will never give up on you."

Fran says sweetly, "Sarah, Mommy and I don't want to give up either. But we don't know what it's like to be you, suffering like this. We want you to know that you have our permission to say, 'Stop.'"

"I will not stop fighting. I will never give up, so don't ever ask me this ever again. I don't want to talk about this ever again."

"OK, Sarah."

I'm so torn up inside. Did we do the right thing talking to her about this or have we just upset her unnecessarily?

## Sarah

I knew I was dying even before Mommy told me. I never told her, because I didn't want to scare her, but now she knows, too. The doctors told her. I still have hope that the lungs will come in time, but I am not certain anymore.

The thought of dying terrifies me. I don't want to die. I believe in God and heaven, but I'm afraid to go there, because Mommy and Daddy aren't there.

My cousin Jack-Jack died of brain cancer when he was four and I was six. I've always been scared that Jack-Jack didn't have his mommy and brother Robby in heaven. How could he be happy there alone? It gave me nightmares; it still gives me nightmares.

Ever since Jack-Jack died, Mommy and Daddy have talked to me a lot about heaven. They would say, "God loves you even more than a mommy or daddy," but that's hard to imagine. My mommy also says that her mommy, my grandma, is there taking care of Jack-Jack and that she's the best mommy in the world. But I want *my* mommy. None of this makes me less scared right now.

I'm not as afraid of the pain of dying, because it's hard to imagine feeling much worse than I do now. I'm terrified to not have my mommy and daddy or my sibs or my cousins. I don't want to leave my family. I'm so scared!

I guess I started to figure it out right before we came down to the scary floor. I just keep getting worse and worse. I can't even maintain my oxygen levels with a nasal cannula anymore, no matter how many liters flow through it. I need a BiPAP machine, and I can see that they keep adjusting the settings on that, too. More and more, I know that my machines are doing the work of breathing, not me.

All day long, I vomit over and over again even though I'm not eating. Mom sits up with me for hours rubbing my back while I retch. My stomach hurts so bad. I am miserable. We put on a *Baby Einstein* video, which helps me relax even when I am in terrible pain. It's soothing. I try to breathe evenly to calm my stomach. The pain is just too much to take.

I can barely get out of bed to use the bathroom. I am so weak. I feel like I will collapse from the smallest effort.

I have shooting pains in my back now, too. The doctors did an X-ray and say I broke parts of it. It's what's called *compression fractures*. How do you break your back sitting in bed? It makes no sense to me.

But I knew things were really bad when I started to see Jack-Jack. I would see him sitting in my hospital room watching over me. The worse I got, the more he came. I like that he looks normal and healthy, like before he got sick. He mostly sits with me, but he sometimes talks. He is happy in heaven, which surprises me.

I don't tell Mommy, Daddy, and Aunt Sharon right away that I am seeing Jack-Jack. I know it's not a normal thing to be seeing, and I keep it to myself at first.

One time, when Robby, Jack-Jack's brother, is visiting me, Jack-Jack appears. I don't tell Robby. Jack-Jack looks very happy to see Robby. I've missed Jack-Jack so much.

At this point, I'm really just terrified. I love Jack-Jack, but as much as I love seeing him, I don't want to go to heaven and be with him forever, not yet. I'm only ten! I want to grow up and do all the things you are supposed to do.

I am not ready to give up. I'm not there yet. This might not be easy, but if I could just get lungs, it would be possible; my future, growing up, might be possible. I'll hold on to that.

# 3. Third Chance

Emotionally rocked, we try to put the morning behind us. My sisters, Lora and Sharon, come and help us. Sarah's mood always soars when they are here. We are an extremely close family. And there are very few people I want in the room right now. It's just too hard to handle other people's emotions; Fran and I are barely hanging on.

And then it happens. Sarah's nurse practitioner, Katie, asks Fran and me to step into the hallway. She is grinning from ear to ear, and I know we got the call! Butterflies fill my stomach. My heart is racing.

"We have an offer!" Katie says. I want to scream, but instead I squeeze Katie tight as excitement fills my veins. More than anyone else on the team, Katie has walked this road with us. She is our partner. We would be lost without her. We walk to the family lounge, Fran and I hand in hand, to learn the details.

"It's a pediatric match. It looks good, but we are in the very early stages. Given Sarah's dire situation, we will likely accept the offer even if tests reveal the lungs aren't perfect," explains Katie.

In that moment, every emotion floods me: utter relief for Sarah and complete despair for this other family that is now living my worst fear. "I think you should not tell Sarah," Katie explains. "There's no reason she has to know until the very last minute." Fran and I completely agree.

We have gotten the call before, twice, and both times ended in what is called a "dry run." The disappointment is hard to handle for an adult, let alone for Sarah. She's very afraid to go into that operating room. The anticipation is horrible. But this time, my fear is not about the operation. I fear it will be another dry run, and that Sarah won't live to see another offer.

My sisters sit and wait with us. We play Monopoly with Sarah, of course. At times, she seems less lucid than at other times. Her carbon dioxide ($CO_2$) levels are creeping up, and this can make her confused and loopy. Finally, close to midnight, Sarah falls asleep.

The four of us pour glasses of wine and wait, and wait, for the final call telling us that it's a go. This is it. It would take a catastrophic problem with the lungs for the team to turn them down. They know we are unlikely to get another offer in time to save Sarah.

When we received our first offer of pediatric lungs in October 2012, Sarah had been on the transplant list for about ten months. She was still living at home, and her health was relatively stable. We had worked hard to keep it that way. She was getting about four hours of chest physical therapy a day to help lift the thick, sticky, infected mucus in her lungs. We went to pulmonary rehab several times a week to keep her strong and fit for transplant. Our lives revolved around keeping Sarah healthy and strong. I am overprotective, so Sarah never left my sight.

The year before Sarah was listed for lungs, Fran and I began the adoption of a sweet, precious eight-year-old girl from Ghana. The process of bringing Ella home went at a snail's pace, with every delay and problem imaginable. But finally, the moment had arrived; it was time for Ella to come home. Sarah, who had been relatively healthy when we began the adoption process, was now ten months into waiting for a lung transplant.

Since I was the one who had met Ella on previous visits to Ghana, Fran and I agreed she would feel safest coming home with me. Torn between my two daughters, I packed up and headed off for ten days in Ghana with my mother-in-law, Jacquie. Fran took time off from work and became Sarah's full-time caregiver. The plan seemed like a good one.

So, there I was, about six days into my trip, in my hotel room in West Africa, and it happened. Sarah got the call for lungs.

I woke up to several missed calls on my cell phone, and I panicked. Fran did not call me when I was in Ghana. He is a man who worries about money—a lot—and calling Africa was too big of an expense if there wasn't a good reason. So, having several missed calls from him was scary.

When I finally got through to him, I got the news that Sarah had received the call. I was in a panic. Of course, this was what we had prayed for and waited on desperately for the last ten months, but I had pictured holding her hand, being by her side. I felt like a failure. I had left her when she needed me the most.

Jacquie and I decided quickly: I would fly home to Sarah, and she would stay in Ghana with Ella. I knew this was a scary thought for Jacquie—alone in West Africa, trying to navigate the visa process and take care of her new granddaughter who spoke only a little English. I knew this would confuse Ella and make her heart worry that I was abandoning her. It was not ideal, but there were no other good choices. Jacquie did not hesitate.

Then, just as we had agreed on a plan, Fran called and told us it was a dry run.

## Lora (Sarah's Aunt)

I had been on call for almost a year since Sarah went on the transplant list in December 2011, but I was completely unprepared for that first call. On the night of the first dry run, I accidentally left the ringer on my cell phone turned off and didn't hear my house phone ringing downstairs. Sharon tried numerous times to call me before she resorted to calling my neighbor. So, I ended up being woken by my neighbor banging on my front door in the middle of the night.

When I stumbled downstairs and opened the front door, my neighbor blurted out, "Sarah got lungs!" I stood there for a moment, uncomprehending, and then called Sharon. It had been decided I would meet Sarah and Fran at the hospital while Sharon stayed home with her and Janet's kids. I ran upstairs, got dressed, and drove to the hospital.

When I got to Sarah's room at CHOP, I found Sarah in bed, excited and nervous. I sat on the bed with her. I had only been there about fifteen minutes when Fran stepped into the hall and got the news that the lungs were a no-go. Fran came back into the room and told us the lungs weren't good enough. Sarah asked why, and we explained that the lungs were not healthy enough for transplant. Sarah turned to me and said, "Aunt Lora, I'm not doing dry runs in the middle of the night. I'm only coming in the middle of the night for the real thing."

My reaction to that first offer of lungs that didn't work out was different from my reaction to the other experiences we had with dry runs. It was almost a relief that she wouldn't be having her transplant without her mom in the country. And I was still very optimistic that there would be more offers. How naive I was.

And then, believe it or not, it happened again—just a few days later, with us still in Ghana! It was a Wednesday. We had gone to the embassy on Monday and been approved for the visa to take Ella home, but we did not have the paperwork in hand yet. It would be ready Friday.

Fran said the team was optimistic but had asked him to wait at home until the offer was more solidified. A couple of hours later, with the good news that these lungs so far looked great, Fran, Sarah, and Sharon were heading to the hospital. It was going to happen this time. Frantic and tearful, Jacquie and I hailed a cab and whisked Ella to the U.S. embassy.

At the entrance to the U.S. embassy in Ghana, I was met with an unwilling guard, who wanted no part of me entering without an appointment. I was hysterical and demanding.

"I am an American citizen. This is my embassy, and I have an emergency. You cannot deny me entrance!" I screamed at this poor guard just trying to do his job. He argued with me, but there's no stopping a mama on a mission. It eventually worked, and I ran in frantic.

As I approached the agent, I tried to compose myself, which was laughable, because I was unhinged. When I finally got to the counter, I burst into tears.

"Please help me," I sobbed. Then I broke into a long explanation of my crazy life. By the end of my story, the agent was crying, too.

"Hold on, and I'll see what I can do," she said, very determined.

Over the next hour, the U.S. embassy rushed Ella's paperwork, and we walked out with her visa in hand.

By the time we exited the embassy, my sister Lora had us booked on a flight home to the United States for that night. I would be there when Sarah woke up from her transplant.

Ella was beaming. Yes, she found it concerning that her mommy was so upset. Certainly, she could tell that I was a bit of a wreck.

But at that moment, she understood she was getting on a plane that very night and going home to her new family—finally. She was ecstatic. The three of us finally got through a long and grueling customs process and were boarding the plane when Fran called.

"It's another dry run," he said, his voice full of disappointment. Sadness enveloped me.

## Sarah

I couldn't believe it. Mommy's away in Ghana, I've had *no* offer for lungs for ten months; then Mommy goes away for the first time, and I get not one but two offers! I knew I wanted new lungs; I wanted to run and play like other kids, to go to school, but my mommy was gone. I needed her. This couldn't happen without Mommy. I was really scared and upset.

The second call seemed like the real thing. We went to the hospital, and Aunt Sharon came in Mommy's place. By the time we arrived, I was panicked. My friend Kate, a child-life specialist, sat with me, and we began an epic art project involving lots of glitter. She always had great crafts and was good at distracting me when I needed it. I definitely needed it then.

I did start to feel better. I was on 8-South, which is where kids with CF are hospitalized. It's a warm and friendly place with lots of doctors and nurses who've known me my whole life. Everyone was pretty excited for me.

Daddy spent a lot of time talking to doctors, making decisions. Aunt Sharon sat in bed snuggling me. She promised me lots of toys when I woke up with my new lungs. She's good at distracting me, too.

Maybe I *could* do this without Mommy. It's not what I wanted, but I started to think I could do it. I started to hope it was not another "fake transplant"—that's what I called the dry runs. Now that I knew this was even a thing.

Daddy said Mommy was at the U.S. embassy getting Ella's paperwork and that she would be home before I even woke up from the transplant. I would have new lungs and a new sister. You gotta admit, that's pretty amazing!

So here we are, eighteen months into the wait for lungs—eight months after those first two dry runs. At this moment, those dry runs are weighing heavily on me. We finally have our third offer for lungs, and it's on the same day we learned Sarah is at the end of her ability to wait. I can barely breathe. We need these lungs. If this is another dry run, we will most likely lose Sarah. The four of us wait quietly, hopefully.

Just after midnight, the transplant team calls. They are at the hospital with the donor, and the lungs look good. We are a go for transplant! I just lie in bed holding Sarah while she sleeps, crying tears of joy and relief.

But just an hour later, we receive a very different call. The donating family cannot move forward. Multiple teams are there to retrieve organs—it's not just Sarah—but this is about this family and their precious baby, too, and they just can't do it. It is just too much for them. And I get it. I grieve for this mother.

I know in my heart that our last chance is lost. We now know that being on the twelve-and-over list, the adult list, means nothing. Sarah is on that list in name only. She has no greater odds of receiving the call today than she did eighteen months ago because she is just ten and three-quarters and not twelve years old. The severity of her illness does not calculate into the decision. Sarah will die.

My heart is broken into a million pieces. I will never be OK again.

# 4. Sarah's Dying Again

I'm paralyzed emotionally. I can't see a way forward. I always told myself that if I did everything right, if I followed all the rules, all the time, that Sarah would live. But now, for the first time, I fear I am preparing for her death. I never truly believed I would be here. It is a soul-crushing feeling. The darkness that surrounds me is so complete. I always believed she would survive. Now, I just don't know.

The PICU doctors come into our dark, dismal room this morning and tell us we will be moving to a different room. This is welcome news. The new room is large, with a lot of exterior light and a beautiful view—perfect for a long-term patient like Sarah. But that's not the only reason they are moving her. The PICU at CHOP is huge, and the doctors say they have several of their most severe patients along this area of the unit because clustering these patients improves their response time in an emergency. Now, they would like Sarah there, too. The message here is not lost on me: they expect a crisis. So, paralyzed and crushed, we begin, once again, to move. It's become hard to hold my head high, to be Sarah's rock, but I am doing it one minute at a time.

"Sarah, we are getting a bright, beautiful new room. I just walked past it, and it's gorgeous." I'm trying hard to be cheerful and focus on the good things with Sarah. She still does not know that we had an offer for lungs last night. She still has hope.

Someone special is coming to help with the move to our new room. Mike McBride, PhD, is an exercise physiologist who rehabs the most severe cardiac and lung transplant patients. His plan is to get Sarah to walk, not be wheeled, to her new room today. Dr. Mike, as Sarah calls him, has been working with Sarah, along with the cystic fibrosis physical therapists (PTs), since her admission to keep her in as good condition as possible for transplant. They all care about Sarah in a personal way, but Sarah's relationship with Dr. Mike is special.

"Sarah, Dr. Mike is coming this morning. He thinks you might like getting out of your room and walking to your new digs. What do you think?" I say hopefully.

"Mommy, I really don't think I can walk. My legs are tired and my back hurts so bad, like shooting pains when I try to stand. Please don't make me. I'm just too tired, and I hurt too much," Sarah says sadly.

It's heartbreaking to be pushing her at this point. My heart is not sure I can do it anymore with so little hope left. I want her to hold on to any little bit of comfort and happiness she can find.

As we have gotten closer to the end of our battle against CF, our experience with physical therapists has been mixed. People we love, who have worked great with Sarah in the past, are now struggling to help her effectively. Sarah can do very little, and this is met with a mixed approach that is not always contributing to Sarah's success. The physical therapists seem to fall into one of two categories. They either do not truly see that she is dying, or they see all too clearly that she is dying. Both perceptions affect the way they care for Sarah.

The physical therapists who don't see how close Sarah is to

dying or just how far she has deteriorated get frustrated when she cries, "I can't!" This makes Sarah feel tremendous shame, as if she is the problem, as if she is just giving up. They admonish us at times. If they had walked our path, they would know that the idea that we aren't trying hard enough could not be further from the truth. But they haven't walked with us long enough to know this, and they inadvertently shame her and me.

The physical therapists who can see Sarah is dying often have such tremendous empathy and sadness for Sarah, that when she cries, "I can't!" they agree internally and leave her in bed. They think we are doomed. And maybe we are, but Sarah sees this, too, the defeat, and feels confirmation of her innermost fear—that she will not get better, that there is no point in trying.

While both these types of therapists come from places of compassion, neither will lead to success with Sarah. She needs something else.

Dr. Mike gets Sarah, and he pushes her in a way no one else seems capable of. The fact that Sarah is near death is not lost on him, but I think most of Dr. Mike's patients are in similar situations. He's funny and kind with Sarah. He has empathy and compassion because he knows what she is going through is truly awful. But that empathy and compassion do not stop him from pushing Sarah; he pushes her more, not less, because she is dying. He finds her limit and takes her to it every time. When Sarah cries, "I can't!" Dr. Mike's attitude is, "It's OK to think you can't, but I have enough faith that you can for both of us, so let's do this."

At times—most of the time—she finds this infuriating, but after every session with Dr. Mike, she is happier and prouder of herself. He is, without a doubt, one of Sarah's favorite people at CHOP, yet he's also the person she fights with the most. She will scream at him sometimes. This morning, Dr. Mike arrives just when they are transferring our room.

"Sarah's not going to sit in bed and be rolled to her new room. She's walking there," he declares emphatically.

"No, I'm not! My stomach hurts. I have a terrible pain in my back. I can't walk there," Sarah firmly replies as she glares at him.

Somehow, though, just moments later, she is up. In true warrior fashion, Sarah drapes a purple cape given to her by a sweet friend of ours over her shoulders and begins to slowly and carefully walk to her new room with Dr. Mike's support and a team following with all her equipment. She makes it to the door of the new room and almost collapses. Dr. Mike gets her the rest of the way. I'm amazed she made it so far, and so is she.

### Sarah

When I first met Dr. Mike over a year ago, I did not like him at all. I can remember the day crystal clearly, like it was yesterday. I had been inpatient for over a week, and I had gotten really sick. Sick enough that I had landed back on the scary floor, instead of my beloved 8-South with all my nurse friends and respiratory therapists. Anyway, I felt awful—fevers, vomiting, oxygen, CPAP—pretty much the worst.

And then, what do you know, in waltzes Dr. Mike. I had never met him before, and he says we are going to take a "trip" to his gym to exercise. He is pumped! Seriously, I had not been out of my bed, except to go to the bathroom, in days. He said that was the point. Then he suggested that I walk to this far-away gym, and I can tell you, I really started to hate that man.

I fought with him about walking. I mean, couldn't he see I was in no shape to go to the gym anyway? And clearly, if I walked, I certainly would not be exercising also. He finally agreed to wheel me down.

But once I got there, he had big plans for me. Up on the treadmill I got, and when I started to cry with exhaustion, he finally let me sit down. As I started to catch my breath, he plopped weights in my hands, and I thought, *Aren't we done?* No, we weren't. Well, I won't give you all the details, but I cried and yelled, and yet somehow I kept lifting weights.

This is not the story of how I came to love Dr. Mike; it's just our bad beginning, and thinking back, I do not remember the moment in time when my feelings changed, but they did. Now, he feels like my partner, like we are climbing this mountain together, and he will be damned if we are going to fail. That is clearly not an option.

So, today, while I feel horrible and I make my angry faces and complain, I know I am getting out of that bed and walking when he says I am.

Even simple acts like standing scare me now. My legs feel very wobbly. I do not think I can walk at all, but there is no sense telling Dr. Mike this. So, I put on my purple CF Warrior cape so that I feel brave, and I go one step at a time. And I truly cannot believe that I am actually doing it (well, most of it), but I never quit. I do feel very proud of myself; I always do after I see Dr. Mike.

When we get to the new room, it's bright and cheery—huge, even—just like Mommy described it. It's still not 8-South, though, so it is hard to get excited about the upgrade. I miss my people.

The new room is bright and gorgeous with plenty of space and sunshine. It lifts my mood initially. Once again, we begin redecorating, trying to bring happiness to Sarah's life. I know the vast room is a virtual operating room and is spacious for that reason, but I am good at blocking this thought—at least I am right up until the large orange box appears. I'm told the box needs to remain in the room, untouched; that it is a crash kit that will allow them to intubate her at a moment's notice. It's hard to hear these things and then put them aside with that bright orange box staring you right in the face.

It's a long day, and Sarah seems a lot less well by the end of it. The biggest change is that she has moments where she seems totally confused, and she wants to sleep all the time. The doctors are routinely pulling blood and looking at her blood gas. The less lucid she is, the closer we get to intubation. I know the number they are looking for, and I wait on those results with bated breath. Every day, every hour we can put off intubation is a small victory.

As night falls, just a few rooms away, the horror begins. Doctors call a code blue. The entire hospital, it seems, descends on the room. It's a family we've met in passing. I've seen the mom crying in the hallway; we've hugged. Her daughter—I'll call her Julie for privacy—was in some type of ATV accident and is clinging to life. It appears to me, but I don't really know, that she has a severe head injury.

The family reminds me of my family. They've taken over the family lounge, sleeping on couches and the floor, not leaving their girl. The parents are standing vigil by her side. This must be what hell looks like—her parents standing in horror outside her room as doctors struggle to keep their baby alive.

After what seems like hours, Julie seems to stabilize. I feel like I can breathe again. I go to the family waiting room to get something out of the fridge, and I hear her family talking. The doctors want to run tests. I worry that Julie may be brain-dead. When I pass by her room on my way back to our room, they are wheeling her bed out. Her mom is in the hallway, and she looks paralyzed, like me. We hug each other in silence; there's nothing to say.

# 5. Deciding to Fight

I am choosing to live as if tomorrow will never come. I live hour to hour, minute to minute. Tomorrow cannot exist in my mind anymore, because when it does, when I acknowledge tomorrow, I know there may be no Sarah. And then I will fall apart. I do not have the luxury of falling apart. I need to be the person Sarah needs me to be right now—joy, comfort, love. I need to fight, and I cannot fight and fall apart at the same time. Each single moment is all that matters.

*Please, God, stay, be with me, do not leave me alone. Please, God, carry me. I cannot do this alone. We cannot do this alone,* I am begging in my mind as I lie in the hospital bed and hold my girl. Sarah's hands are soft and warm. Her hair is so long now and smooth as silk. I love stroking it and breathing her in. She sleeps heavily and for long hours as the carbon dioxide building in her bloodstream slowly poisons her. When I hug her or kiss her, she doesn't even stir, so I do so constantly.

In the PICU, they talk about patients getting their days and nights confused, causing a type of psychosis. I totally understand this. Here, day goes into night and night into day with barely any differentiation. The doctors come in as regularly at two in the morning as they do at four in the afternoon. On the general floors, like our beloved 8-South, they try to leave patients alone at night. The level of care Sarah needs now makes that impossible.

The focus at this point has become Sarah's blood work. We are waiting and watching for that moment when it is no longer safe for her to be alert and with us. Intubation will give the doctors more direct access to her lungs and allow them to oxygenate her better. Fellows come in every few hours like clockwork and draw blood. The next step—intubation—will be perpetual sleep, machines taking over until the end. The end is in sight, and this I cannot face.

I don't leave the room at all anymore, at least not beyond the hallway right in front of it. I seldom shower. I barely sleep. There's no self-care anymore. In this dire situation, I must talk myself into using the bathroom that is located right in her hospital room. I am terrified she will need me and that, in that one moment, I will not be there for her and she will be alone and scared. This thought terrifies me. It is critical that I be there when she needs me.

Truth be told, I have never been good about leaving Sarah when she is in the hospital. But now I have taken this to new levels. For the last three months (since February), Sarah has been inpatient continuously and, therefore, so have I. One night a week, Fran and I alternate, and I go home to the other kids and Fran stays with Sarah, but this is extremely hard for me to do. Fran is more than capable of caring for Sarah in the hospital. The issue is more about my inability to leave her. As much as I miss my other three children—and I do in a way that causes me physical pain— I know Sarah needs me the most, so this is where I have to be. Now, with Sarah so close to dying, Fran and I are both here full-time.

I worry about Sarah's brother Sean the most. He's an emotional wreck with me gone. He cries on the phone to me every time I call. It always starts out the same, almost euphoria to be talking to me, he's on a high, and then utter despair that I am not there. I don't know if it's better to talk to him more or talk to him less. Nothing's the same without me there, he says, and he wants to know "When will Sarah be all better? When will we be together as a family again?" It's heartbreaking not to be able to answer these questions. Before the PICU, the kids would visit all together every weekend, and I'd spend a weekend night at home while Fran stayed with Sarah; so, once a week we'd at least be a family all together in the hospital room. We would even celebrate birthdays this way. So far, both Ella's and Sean's birthdays have been celebrated in a hospital room at CHOP. During the week, we would do special one-on-one visits with each of the kids at the hospital, but now the risk to Sarah is just too high; catching a simple head cold could literally kill her, so we can't take those chances. The kids are now at Sharon's house full-time, and she's trying so hard to manage Sean. Nothing she's doing, or I am saying, is filling the pit of despair for Sean, and it's all spilling over into his life at school, too. I feel so helpless that there's nothing I can do for him.

Finn, on the other hand, seems so unfazed I worry he's completely bonded with a new family and moved on. I know he's just four, but I worry in the opposite way—that he's so young that he's now just totally confused about who his siblings are versus cousins and who his parents are. Ella is sad but tries not to show it or make life harder for anyone else, which is its own problem.

Today, I am exhausted from a night of constantly being woken by beeping monitors and false alarms. My sister Sharon, who has been holding down the fort at home with our combined seven children, is here now. Lora will be here later today as well. They are both putting their lives and families on hold to support us. Everyone knows this is it; we are at the end.

Sharon is a single mom, and Claire Tierney—Sharon's nanny and one of our best friends—is taking over at Sharon's house, which is making all this support possible. Claire is a full-time teacher and technically only a part-time nanny, but she is stepping in for us in a major way right now. I don't know how Claire is managing, but she never complains or acts like it's a struggle. She's told me that many friends and neighbors are jumping in to help as well. Fran and I are both very disconnected from the details of our home life right now.

## Sharon (Sarah's Aunt)

On the face of it, the under-twelve rule seems like an obvious injustice, but initially, I think they must have some rationale for this approach. Maybe there are enough pediatric lungs, and it is fair. Maybe kids can somehow wait a little longer for lungs and still survive.

The rules governing transplant are decided by the Organ Procurement and Transplantation Network (OPTN) and the United Network for Organ Sharing (UNOS), which work under contract with the Health Resources and Services Administration of the U.S. Department of Health and Human Services.

I turn to their website for data. My first analysis shows that kids are dying at twice the rate of adults. I am stunned. I check and recheck the calculation. I look at more tables of data. Kids are waiting longer for lungs. A much smaller percentage of children are receiving lungs. And many are dying. It's unbelievable!

I know if we fight this, it may be too late for Sarah, but what if it isn't too late? With shocking regularity, Sarah's situation deteriorates, but somehow, she holds on. Maybe she can hang on long enough for us to fight this injustice.

———

When Sharon arrives, it is clear she is anxious to talk. I have not seen her since our third dry run forty-eight hours before. Now, the two of us take a break outside Sarah's room on a long, thin bench that lines the bustling hallway. Julie's room is still swarming with family. I wonder what her tests showed. Her family looks like they are in despair. I feel like I am watching my future.

"I've barely slept the past two days," Sharon says. "I've poured myself into research, and I think we can fight these laws that are keeping Sarah from getting lungs. There's a huge statistical difference between the survival of kids under twelve and everyone over twelve. It's not an equitable system."

"How big is the difference?" I ask.

"Kids under twelve are dying at almost twice the rate as everyone else waiting for lungs."

My thoughts spill out in a rush. "Oh my God! Are you sure? What should we do? Do we need a lawyer?" It's the first glimmer of hope, and that is all I need, just a speck.

"Yes, I'm sure. A lawyer is what I thought, too. I called my friend Erin, who is a lawyer, and she suggested that filing a lawsuit will take too much time. She thought we should go to 'the court of public opinion' and apply pressure on the OPTN. It's not just Sarah; all kids under twelve are being disadvantaged by their system."

My mind is racing as I absorb what she is saying. I know Sharon would not give me false hope; she would never suggest I do this unless the statistics were real.

"Janet, this is the way I look at it. We can sit here and love and support Sarah quietly, peacefully, until the end. There's nothing wrong with that."

I nod, a million thoughts racing through my head.

"Or we can fight, publicly and loudly. It'll be hard, and we will likely lose Sarah either way, but what if we could save her? What if we could save other kids, too?" she says urgently.

This moment is surreal. I don't need time to think this through. There may be two paths here, but I only see one.

"Yes, we fight! If there's even a slim chance that we could save Sarah, save other kids, then we fight."

## Fran

I make a run for non-cafeteria food, and the reality of what is happening is now fully sinking in, and it is terrible. The fact that Sarah is dying is now staring me in the face. I would pray, but I am too angry. A favorite poet of mine once wrote, "Why do I smile at people I would much rather kick in the eye?" Yep, that is how I feel.

As the day goes on and I wallow in self-misery, I just get angrier at the injustice of the bureaucratic system—rules and regulations are preventing Sarah from getting her proper space in the transplant line. I don't expect her to be allowed to butt in line, only to be allowed to get in line.

Then Sharon tells us what she has learned and that we have the options of sitting quietly with Sarah and watching her die or going out swinging. The choice is crystal clear, not because I am angry but because Sarah was clear with us that we were *never allowed to give up on her!* If Sarah is going to continue fighting that hard, then I am going to stand behind her right to live. And so, at what is possibly the end, this day becomes the beginning.

For the next several hours, Sharon, Fran, and I pore over the data Sharon has collected. Lora has arrived and has joined in helping with Sarah. God, what would I do without them? The four of us rotate so that Sarah is always being loved and doted on. We are careful not to discuss things in front of her. We brainstorm and come up with a plan.

Around 10:00 P.M., Sharon heads home to draft the email that I will send to all my friends in "the business." My background is in journalism—before I became a stay-at-home mom to Sarah. For several years after college, I worked as a news producer, and for the last couple of years before Sarah's birth, I was a public relations executive at a local PR and advertising firm. Some of my favorite people still work in PR, particularly a group of strong, fierce girlfriends, fellow moms. I turn to them now.

It's funny, because for years I often wished I had made different choices. Specifically, I found myself needing to be a nurse to this fragile little girl, and I wished I actually was one. I wondered, just a bit, why God couldn't have guided me a little better—a nursing or medical degree would have been a far more useful background than public relations. Little did I know how all the dots would connect.

Sometime after midnight, in bed next to Sarah with Fran by my side, I send the email out to several friends, and like wildfire it spreads.

*May 24, 2013/Friday*

*Dear friends from my former PR life,*

*Sarah needs your help. She has only a week or two before she will lose her battle with Cystic Fibrosis if she does not receive donor lungs. If Sarah was 12 years old, she would have a high probability of receiving lungs in time. Since she is 10, she will only receive adult donor lungs after all adult candidates, regardless of how sick they are, have the opportunity to accept donor lungs. We need to draw national attention to this arbitrary ruling which costs children their lives. I need your ideas and efforts to make this happen quickly. Lawyers we have consulted recommend a PR battle is the best hope.*

*This is a policy created by the Organ Procurement and Transplantation Network (OPTN), the nation's organ procurement donation and transplantation system and enforced through United Network for Organ Sharing (UNOS), which manages the US organ transplant system under contract with the federal government.*

*Based on a 2000 ruling by the US Department of Health and Human Services, which mandated that organ allocation policies must be based on medical necessity rather than waiting time, OPTN implemented a new allocation system based on the severity of a patient's illness (the Lung Allocation Score, or LAS), rather than the amount of time served on the wait list in 2005. This reduced the number of deaths among patients awaiting lung transplant, ensured lungs were allocated to those with less stable diagnoses, and dramatically reduced the average wait time from over 2 years, and reduced the wait list by half. This new approach only applied to patients over the age of 12.*

*This approach was not extended to children. Despite the fact that many pediatric patients can use a partial lobar transplant from an adult donor, these young patients are only offered adult donor lungs after all adult patients, regardless of the severity of the child's illness. While Sarah has an LAS score over 60, which would normally place her as the highest priority for her blood type in the region, all adults in the region with her blood type will be offered the lungs first, even those with more stable diagnoses and lower LAS scores. Sarah will only be offered adult lungs if no adult candidates accept the organ.*

*Sarah is a top priority on the pediatric list, but the pediatric donors are far fewer than the adult donors, dramatically reducing the number of lungs Sarah is offered. So far in 2013, there were 1,133 adult deceased lung donors and only 70 under the age of 12. The result is only 4 pediatric lung donor recipients in 2013, and 291 for those over 12 years old.*

*This policy needs to change. The Lung Review Board, a national group of transplant physicians and surgeons, can make an exceptional ruling for Sarah. And they can recommend new policies to OPTN. Luis Angel is the Chair of the Lung Review Board (UT School of Medicine San Antonio).*

*I need your help to get this story on the national stage. Only with substantial pressure will we get Sarah considered for lungs based on the severity of her illness not her age.*

*Please let me know if you can help!*

*Janet*

Tears streaming down my face, I close my computer and snuggle up to Sarah in bed. Fran is on the cot next to me in the room. Sarah is sleeping soundly, tubes and wires everywhere. I hold her warm, soft body in my arms, stroking her hair as I drift off to sleep. I will never, ever give up on her. This is not over, not by a long shot.

## Sarah

Mommy, Daddy, and Aunt Sharon are talking a lot in the hallway tonight. I don't know what that's about, but it makes me nervous. Is something more wrong? I'm so tired that I keep falling asleep. I want to stay awake and ask them what's going on, but I just can't keep my eyes open.

When I wake back up, it's just me and Jack-Jack in the room. I'm happy to see him again, but instead of just sitting quietly, I take the chance to tell him what's on my mind.

"Jack-Jack, I think I am coming to heaven soon. I need you to make my room up. Please get ready for me, because I am really scared," I tell him while crying. I'm relieved to finally be alone long enough to tell him this.

But Jack-Jack surprises me. "No, Sarah, it's not your time yet. We have a plan, and you are not coming to heaven. You need to be brave and fight a little longer. Can you do that?"

"Yes, I can do that!"

I'm so happy that I am going to live. I really didn't want to leave everyone. The thought terrifies me. I just cry. I can't wait to tell Aunt Sharon. Jack-Jack has a plan.

I can barely keep my eyes open. I will tell them when I wake. I am going to live. I am going to fight. I am going to get lungs. If Jack-Jack said it, then I know it's true.

# 6. Going Public

I wake up to my baby sleeping heavily again, almost comatose. I brush my teeth, pull my hair into a ponytail, and step outside the room to do rounds with the enormous team of doctors headed my way. I slept in bed with Sarah, jumping at every beep, every alarm. It's about seven in the morning, and the halls have this eerie, quiet feeling, like the calm before the storm. Fran and I look like hell.

Each morning, the doctors do rounds at CHOP. It's a teaching hospital, and in the PICU, the rounds can be quite extensive. Usually, at least ten doctors plus nurses, maybe more, come to discuss Sarah's dire situation and agree on a plan of action.

Sarah's team has widened as her complications have grown. It now includes a cardiologist, because although Sarah's heart is typically strong and normal, the enormous pressure her failing lungs have placed on them has caused pulmonary hypertension. So, we are watching her for heart failure now, too. Just the thought sends chills down my spine.

This is a whole new specialty, and the terminology is foreign to me. I've taken to Google research, which is just about the worst thing you can do when you are in a medical crisis and frightened—worst fears confirmed. What if we end up needing a heart-lung transplant?

Sarah's cardiologist is considered the best of the best when it comes to pulmonary hypertension, but he speaks way above my head, and I know I am not comprehending all the details. I have had ten years to learn CF. I've had days to grasp pulmonary hypertension. To make matters more interesting, he is a quirky guy, who I imagine Sarah would very much enjoy if she were ever awake and with it enough to meet him, but this only makes conversations with him more confusing. I wish this whole nightmare would disappear. If only one of those transplants eight months ago had not been a dry run, how different our lives would look right now.

"So, Sarah's BNP is slightly lower than yesterday, a positive indicator that the heart is hanging on," he states to the team as much as to me as he rattles on a bunch of other details.

*Positive indicator,* I think.

"So, are you saying that Sarah's heart looks better today?" I'm pleased to finally be getting some good news, or so I think.

"Uh, yeah, I guess I'm saying that. It's improved, technically, as in millimeters to the sun."

*Millimeters to the sun,* I'm thinking. What the hell kind of description is that? Good Lord, speak English, people. I have not slept in days.

I can feel myself almost holding my breath as the team discusses her heart, willing myself to just breathe. "So, do we think the heart will be able to rebound post-transplant?" another attending questions.

*Please say yes, please say yes,* I think.

"Yes, there's nothing wrong with *my* heart," he says, meaning Sarah's heart. "*My* heart is not the problem; *your* lungs are the problem," he tells the pulmonologists. The doctors move on, and I can feel the tension release; I start to breathe again.

The rest of rounds are a blur, and I walk back into Sarah's room feeling beaten down, alone, and depressed. It's a paralyzing, hopeless feeling that makes me want to curl into a ball and accept defeat. Every fact in front of me says this is the end; there is no hope. I have to force myself forward physically.

Sarah is still sleeping soundly. She will probably sleep until two in the afternoon or even later. It's a relief to be able to walk back into our room without the forced smile and cheerfulness. I need to be able to just *be* for a moment.

I take a deep breath and log on to my computer, wondering if anyone has had a chance to respond to my email. Amazingly, when I open the email chain, there are hundreds of messages. There's a back-and-forth conversation with a plan developing, and dozens of additional people have been added to the conversation. It seems that they have all dropped their Memorial Day weekend plans in a heartbeat for Sarah.

Two of my closest friends, from my work in public relations, are leading this group they will soon coin "Team Sarah": Tracy Simon and Maureen Garrity. The most overwhelming part is that everyone is on board, even friends of friends, who I never worked with or even knew very well at all. I scroll back, trying to catch up with the conversation, tears streaming down my face, but for the first time, they are tears of hope instead of hopelessness. Our little family is not alone anymore! For the first time in a long time, we are not alone. Sarah's army has emerged.

### Tracy Simon

It is the morning of May 24, 2013, and I am in hunting-and-gathering mode for a Memorial Day weekend visit to my mom and dad's new beach house with my husband, Eric, and our girls (ages five and three): snacks for the car, toothbrushes, outfits, bath stuff, sneakers, laptop, dinosaur chicken nuggets, mac and cheese.

Then I see it—the Facebook message from Janet asking her public relations friends for help. Sarah has been on the waiting list for lungs for a year and a half and has been living at CHOP for three months now. Janet's message says that she has discovered a flaw in the country's lung allocation process, and public pressure may be the only thing that can save Sarah. Can we help?

How can this be happening to someone I know? A PR battle to save a child—my friend's child. Far from the noble ranks of police officers, doctors, firefighters, and soldiers, people in public relations do not get to carry out lifesaving missions very often. I am not even sure that anything I do will help, but as a mother, friend, and human being, I must try.

I stop my mind from spinning by focusing on how this story could play out in the news. I'm sure we can get the local media interested, but what about the national media? We need a national story. And we will need some pretty compelling images and interviews from Janet and Fran. What kind of video do they have of Sarah? Can we even get the media into the hospital?

I begin adding names to the Facebook chat Janet started, including other PR colleagues, friends, cousins who are doctors, people who know politicians—anyone and everyone I can think of who might be able to help. The list quickly swells to fifty members.

Janet and her family have done their homework. The disturbing reality of Sarah's urgent condition and the inequalities in the lung transplant policy have been laid out for us. Janet has even included the names of the officials who govern the policy. We have enough information to create a media pitch quickly.

Who can I reach in the national media? Suddenly, I remember seeing on Facebook that a friend from my high school trip to

Israel is now at CNN. I guess it's time to get back in touch. So, while packing the car for the beach, I write one of the sloppiest PR pitches of my life, fueled by adrenaline and riddled with spelling errors. And soon my phone vibrates with a response— by the grace of G-d, he has replied. He says he is interested in the story and says he will pass the information along.

I strap the girls into their car seats and turn on a movie, and off to the beach we go. I have no idea if this national story will even land. During the drive, I learn CNN already has a crew in Philadelphia on another story and will be sending the crew to interview Sarah and her family tonight. Something bigger than I have ever worked on is going down, and my relaxing weekend of sand and sunshine just took a hard turn in another direction— a more important one.

With a renewed excitement and energy, Sharon rallies with me at the hospital. We are working with Maureen now on messaging, and Tracy and a few others have already begun to reach out to the media. It's a rather large team, and we want to make sure the whole group is on the same page. We have zero budget to fight a national battle with the federal government, but the team is entirely confident.

The overall message is a simple one: Sarah has been waiting for eighteen months with end-stage cystic fibrosis for a double lung transplant. She is only weeks away from losing her battle. If she were two years older, she would have a high probability of receiving lungs in time. Sadly, this is not the case. While Sarah's medical team has approved her for lungs from a donor twelve years and older, current rules restrict her access to these organs. Because of her age, and her age alone, Sarah will only receive an offer of organs after all candidates twelve and older in her region, regardless of how sick they are, have the opportunity to accept them or reject them. While Sarah is a top priority for under-twelve lungs, they are few and far between.

These ladies are pros with deep contacts throughout the media, so their pitching of the story is fast and furious, and within hours, I have an interview with *The Philadelphia Inquirer.*

I'm sick to my stomach over the thought of losing Sarah, and that's all that matters to me. It's easier to face the media when you have nothing to lose. I feel like I've got this! I have analyzed the statistics with Sharon; it's undeniable that kids under twelve are being disadvantaged by the system. All the data on survivability is publicly accessible. It is UNOS's own data, and it is clear that kids under twelve are dying at a much higher rate than everyone twelve and over. The difference between ten and twelve in the UNOS system is the difference between life and death. Is there such a huge physical difference between a ten-year-old and a twelve-year-old with cystic fibrosis that Sarah should be allowed to die? The more I understand, the more infuriated I become.

I understand the core problem. There are not enough lungs to go around; there just are not enough donors. Tasked with creating an equitable system, UNOS has divided patients into groups based on what appear to be arbitrary age cutoffs. The problem is that it is not a fair system, not even close. One out of every ten "adults" (people twelve and over) waiting for lungs will die while waiting. Meanwhile, two out of every ten kids under twelve will die waiting. Kids under twelve are dying at twice the rate as patients twelve and over. They know it, and now I'm going to make sure everyone else knows it, too. I don't know how they could possibly defend this, but I am interested to find out.

I have never been so certain about anything as I am about this. It's like everything from my past—Sarah's fast progression with the disease, the three dry runs while waiting, my PR and TV experience—is all colliding into this one rare moment. I have a unique chance to fight a real injustice, to change something, and,

God willing, to save Sarah in the process. It's hard not to see God's miracles weaving a path through this. Sometimes miracles are not the grand moment where the blind person sees or the deaf person hears; they are the little things that lead to that final moment. Miracles are often in the details, I find.

There's nothing like the feeling that you have nothing to lose. That's how I feel right now. The typical butterflies and self-doubt that would normally exist are not there. They just aren't. I have never felt so confident that I was right about something before.

Our first interview is with *The Philadelphia Inquirer*; then we get our first national hit. CNN decides to pick up the story. They are sending a crew from New York. It's Memorial Day weekend and, thankfully, a slow news weekend, and as a former producer, I know *this* slowness will make all the difference as we pitch the story.

I need to let the team at CHOP know my plans; I don't want them blindsided, and they have no idea at this point what I have uncovered and what I am about to do. My PR team reaches out to the hospital PR team while I talk to Dr. Goldfarb and Katie. We know the entire pulmonary team. You don't live in the hospital for three straight months without pretty much knowing them all. Their response is supportive. It seems clear to me that they, too, think there is an injustice happening on the under-twelve list, but they do not come right out and say it. The business side of the hospital, on the other hand, is not jazzed. They have strict media policies—they do not want media in the hospital or on their property—and in the coming weeks, I will try their patience for sure. While talking to the team, I leave Sharon with Sarah.

### Sharon

When I get to CHOP, Jan and Fran need to step out of the room, and I have one of those rare moments alone with Sarah.

She seems alert and excited to see me. We always have a good time together. I've always considered myself the "fun" aunt, and I come armed with toys and games. It's all about distraction at this point.

Today, I am not at all prepared for what Sarah has to say.

"Oh, Aunt Sharon, I wanted to tell you that I saw Jack-Jack," she says casually as she drops what is clearly a bombshell on me.

"You mean you had a dream?" I ask cautiously.

"No," she says. "I saw him. He was here."

As a family, we have always believed Jack was still here with us in his own way. We'd look for signs, and our sign for Jack has always been ladybugs. The story behind it is a favorite among the kids. When Jack was little, we lived in a neighborhood with a sewage treatment facility since we did not have public sewers. One day, when the kids went for a walk with one of the neighborhood dads, he told them that the building was a "poopy factory." He explained that bugs were in the "poopy factory" and that they liked to eat poop. Well, Jack loved this story. From this point forward, every time Jack pooped, he would shout as he flushed the toilet, "Another one for the ladybugs!" It was a riot.

After his death, we began seeing ladybugs at all sorts of special times. The first time was when Robby and I were at Christmas Mass, our first Christmas without Jack, and right there on the pew on a cold winter day was a ladybug crawling along. From this point forward, ladybugs were a sign for us that Jack was with us.

But no one has ever seen Jack in the way Sarah is describing. You always hear stories of people who are close to death seeing loved ones who have passed, and I start to fear that this is a sign we are close to the end. I try my best to remain casual and calm as I respond to Sarah.

"Oh," I say, trying to hide my surprise.

"Do you know what he said, Aunt Sharon?"

"No, what did he say?" I try to keep my voice normal as I respond, as if we are discussing our latest game of Monopoly.

"Well, I told him that I would be with him soon in heaven," she says. This is the first time I realize that Sarah believes she will die. My mind is racing. How do I respond to both of these revelations?

"Do you know what he said, Aunt Sharon?"

"No, I don't," I say as my mind spins.

"He said I would live! He said I wouldn't join him for a long, long time." She's clearly thrilled but also looking to see if I believe her. She wants to know that what she is seeing is real.

"Wow, that's great!" I say, and I mean it. I believe she saw Jack-Jack, and I know now that the pressure is on. Jack-Jack promised, and I intend to keep that promise.

As we prepare for the CNN interview, we are keenly aware that Sarah does not understand what is going on. This is intentional, as we don't want to scare her any more than she is already. I tell Sarah that this nice reporter wants to do a story about her and how brave she is. Sarah's all in.

When CNN reporter Zain Asher and CNN producer Chris Welch arrive, we invite them into Sarah's room. They cannot bring any camera equipment, but they can be my guests. Sarah is awake and animated when Zain and Chris arrive. She's always a bit groggy, but it's not terrible tonight. The plan is for them to interview Sarah using my iPhone and then for Fran and me to go to another location for a more formal interview while my sister Lora stays with Sarah. Sharon will come with us.

As Zain and Sarah talk, I'm struck by how amazing Sarah is. She's just ten but possesses the wisdom of someone much older. By the end of the interview, Zain is in tears, and though I try to hide it, so am I.

The story by Chris Welch and Zain Asher runs, and it captures people's hearts.[1] In the interview, Sarah tells the reporters and—through them—the world what it is like to live with cystic fibrosis.

*Asked how she would describe living with CF, Sarah says to "close your eyes and pretend you're on a boat." The boat she describes represents her lungs.*

*"The water keeps the boat afloat, but sand sinks your boat. And all we got is a little sandy, but we're going to be OK."*

*"She may feel like she's kind of sinking," mom said in a later interview. "As she said, what you can do . . . is kind of brush off the sand, or if you need to get a new boat, kind of start over, which would be a transplant, to get a new set of lungs, so she'd be clean again." But "brushing off her boat" and getting that transplant has proved difficult.*

Sarah also performs a song she wrote from her hospital bed and talks about the life she is looking forward to after her transplant.

*"I used to go to school before I got oxygen," Sarah says, pausing to wipe away tears as the "puffs" from the oxygen mask toss her bangs. "Got to go to school and at least try and act like all the other normal children."*

The story explains that Sarah has been waiting for these new lungs for eighteen months and that she is the number-one candidate on the priority list for children in our region, which includes

---

1. Chris Welch and Zain Asher, "With Just Weeks Left, Sarah Fights the System for Life-Saving Pair of Lungs," CNN, May 27, 2013, https://www.cnn.com/2013/05/27/health/pennsylvania-girl-lungs/index.html.

Delaware, the District of Columbia, Maryland, New Jersey, Pennsylvania, West Virginia, and northern Virginia.

> *But that's where it gets tricky—she tops the list for children's lungs—not adult lungs. For Sarah, a modified adult lung would fit as well.*
>
> *Two weeks ago, Janet and Fran learned that if Sarah were 12, she'd have a much better chance of receiving adult lungs. But since she is 10, she primarily has access to children's lungs, which are in shorter supply.*
>
> *"That's insane," mom said. "It shouldn't be about their age. If she's the sickest person, she should qualify."*

The CNN story explains that in 2012, only ten patients on the pediatric list received lung transplants and points out that there were more than 1,700 adult lung transplants in that same year.

They also quote Stuart Sweet, MD, PhD, a board member at UNOS who helped create the pediatric transplant system. Dr. Sweet is a pediatric pulmonologist and medical director of the lung transplant program at St. Louis Children's Hospital.

> *"It's not a perfect system. There is no perfect system," Sweet said in an interview. "It's the best we can do right now." Sweet said Sarah's story "tugs at his heart" but that if he changed the system for Sarah's advantage, "there's another patient, very likely an adolescent, who gets a disadvantage."*
>
> *"We've built a system that tries to be as fair to everyone as possible."*

It went on to mention that Sarah has been outdoors only twice in the past one hundred days but is determined to make it to transplant.

*As she puts it, "I'm not going for easy—I'm just going for possible."*

*"We will (get them)! I can't wait to take my first breath with new lungs. I can close my eyes right now and imagine it."*

*"Are we gonna quit?" mom asks.*

*Sarah deliberates very briefly. "No!" she shouts at the top of her lungs and slapping the bed with both hands. "I'm never going to quit! Never, never!"*

# 7. The Story Explodes

Walking into that room and discussing my worst fears on camera with the world is traumatic. I have to admit Sarah is dying. I say it out loud for the world to hear. I let everyone into my worst nightmare, my most vulnerable moment. I want nothing more than to spend my days holding Sarah, supporting Sarah, focusing on Sarah. I don't want fame or notoriety. I just want to quietly live my life and care for my kids.

The hardest part is stepping away from Sarah. CNN's interview required me to leave the hospital and be away from her for at least an hour, maybe two. The clock ticks slowly while I am gone. My stomach is sick and I feel shaky, but not from nerves about the interview. *What is she doing? Is she scared? Is she hurting?*

Sarah's not alone, though; my sister Lora is there. I am flooded with doubt—not doubt about my rightness, not doubt about the facts, but doubt that I can actually make a difference. I wonder, *Could these be my last precious moments with Sarah? Am I spending my last precious moments fighting this uphill battle that I am destined to lose? Who am I to think that I can take on the federal government?* Because, let's be honest, that's what I am trying to do here.

## Lora

For several days, I have thought about nothing else except the injustice of Sarah being barred from receiving adolescent or adult lungs even though this is what she needs and what her doctors think is her best option. We have known that if pediatric lungs did not become available in time, Sarah's surgeons could perform a lobar transplantation from an adolescent or adult donor and that they have the expertise to successfully perform this type of lung transplantation. They are confident a lobar transplant would save Sarah's life, and we trust them totally.

So, it is a terrible shock to find out Sarah will not be able to receive a lobar transplant from donors in the adult pool because she is not yet twelve years old (she is less than three months away from turning eleven). While I have been thinking about this injustice and feeling helpless, Sharon has been doing research and has concluded that the UNOS age rule is arbitrary and that Janet and Fran can fight it if they want to. They have decided to fight—for Sarah and for other children in the future who may be in the same position.

Tonight, we have our first interview with a member of the national news media. Two reporters from CNN are coming to visit Sarah in her room and interview her. After that interview, Janet, Fran, and Sharon will do a full interview with the reporters somewhere off hospital property. My job for the night is to sit with Sarah while they are gone for this interview. Being with Sarah is never a job at all, so I feel very lucky.

I arrive at the hospital prior to the CNN reporters' arrival. I am grateful they are interested in Sarah's story but also nervous and uncomfortable about members of the media talking to *my* girl. What will they say? Will they see her as she is—a courageous, strong, sweet girl? I don't want to share her with these reporters and with the world. I want to protect her from public view, but I can't do that if I also want to help save her life.

Janet will be recording the interview on her cell phone since the reporters are not permitted to bring cameras into the hospital. My sisters tell me to sit on the couch/bed by the window and watch quietly, so I position myself there next to a large collection of Mylar balloons with my legs drawn up. Sarah's bed is only a few feet away, and I am trying to stay out of the way. Janet will sit at the foot of Sarah's bed to record the interview.

I'm not supposed to record the interview, but I surreptitiously hold my phone so I can get video of everything Sarah says. I can't help it. I must preserve as much of her as I can. And I am deeply moved by the things Sarah says to the reporters. She has always been wise beyond her years, even though she is also very innocent. When she compares the experience of having CF with being in a boat that has taken on water and is accumulating sand, I am so sad for her that I almost cry.

After the interview, Janet, Fran, and Sharon gather their things, give Sarah big kisses, and remind her that I will be with her the whole time they are gone, which will not be long at all. By the time they leave the room, I am already situated in Sarah's bed next to her, and she is planning what game or craft we should do in our time together. (Sarah never wastes a single moment with any visitor.)

Sarah and I have a good time, and Sarah sings some songs for me that she made up herself. She even made up a song on the spot about me. I was overwhelmed at this and wanted her to sing it again so I could record it, but she was tired. I can't remember the words now, but I remember that they were very specific to our relationship and that they made me feel I was a very special and unique person in her life. I am overwhelmed with love for her.

I'm relieved to see Sarah still awake and happy when I return to the hospital. The somersaults in my stomach subside a little, and I climb into bed with her. She's confused and groggy; the $CO_2$ is building up in her bloodstream and taking her from me slowly. Soon after this night, Sarah will have no recollection of it, no memory of the CNN interview.

Fran and I see all the changes, and we know we must decide what to do next. I want clarity—someone to say, "Choose this path," but the doctors have presented two paths, both leading to unknown futures.

As the next morning arrives, the big question is: Should we consider ambulatory ECMO? Since Dr. Goldfarb described it, I have done my research. I've looked at the videos of people on ambulatory ECMO. I've read the literature. Fran and I have made the painful decision that this medicine is too adult for a ten-year-old, too terrifying, and too experimental in pediatrics. There is no crystal ball here. We are faced with several crappy choices, with incomplete data, and we have to follow our gut instincts.

Now, Fran and I must face rounds with the doctors. The PICU attending doctor begins. "We are looking at intubation within days if not hours. Mom, we'd like to discuss ambulatory ECMO again."

This PICU doctor wants me to go this route. He is head of the ECMO program and a strong proponent. But this is new, especially in pediatric transplant medicine, and Sarah is dying with no hope of ever getting a fair shot at organs.

"I'm not sure there is anything to discuss," I say, tears welling up in my eyes. "Without any real reason to believe we will receive lungs in time, it is just an extension of the torture, and one that will make the end worse. I won't take the chance she suffers greatly at the end to buy myself a few more days. It's not fair to her."

Ambulatory ECMO is when a machine takes over the function of the lungs, circulating and oxygenating all the blood in the body externally without the use of the lungs. It is the "ambulatory" part that we are not interested in. This is a scary machine and procedure, and to be awake on what is essentially bypass and have to exercise would be terrifying to a ten-year-old.

Sarah's a young ten-year-old—sweet, hopeful, and innocent. She is entirely fragile, relying on us physically in almost every way at this point. Her thin arms and legs look like they can barely hold her frame. This is a monumental thing to expect of Sarah and something that we think she is not capable of.

I know even Dr. Goldfarb, whom I trust implicitly, wants us to choose this path, but we can't. He is quietly supportive.

Saying no to this is one of the hardest things I have ever done. I want every second, every moment, with Sarah that I can get. If I thought that our odds of getting organs were good, I would consider it strongly, but our odds are not good.

This is our reality. I am a perpetual optimist, but right now, for Sarah, it is important that I live in reality and make clear decisions that, while fighting for her life, also plan for what her death will be like. If she dies, if, God forbid, we lose her, we are choosing to do so peacefully, without fear. She will die as the innocent, hopeful little girl that she is; we will not rob her of that.

To go from this moment, this gut-wrenching decision, back to my now-public fight is surreal. Sarah's story explodes in the media beyond even my wildest imagination. Her sweet rendition of "Twinkle, Twinkle, Little Star" paired with her courage and her will to live captures the attention of the American people. Local camera crews line the street outside CHOP. We have struck a chord with the American people; they see the injustice.

Before this, I was always a pretty private person. While I had a Facebook account, I did not blog about Sarah. I just was more comfortable with our private battle. My Facebook consisted of 200–300 friends, all of whom I knew in person. I shared Sarah's story with them and asked for prayers, but it was to my friends; it wasn't every detail, and it felt rather personal and private.

Now I am getting hundreds of Facebook friend requests a day. Anxious to have Sarah's story told, I accept everyone and anyone asking. I am flooded with private messages and prayers from strangers, asking how they can help and what they can do. Multiple strangers ask if they can donate a lung to Sarah. It's amazing and overwhelming. I feel lifted up by their prayers and support.

On the flip side, I quickly find out that the media are among my Facebook friends; whatever I post starts appearing on the national news. It's a little disconcerting at first, but I quickly realize that it's an amazing tool to reach out and share Sarah's story— her updates—without having to walk away from her. I feel indebted to Sarah's followers, and I want to update them. Much to my surprise, the public outpouring is lifting me up and willing me forward to fight.

We start receiving tons of mail at the hospital from Sarah's supporters. Whole elementary school classrooms as well as nursing homes make her cards. These are people we have never met. Balloons, stuffed animals, crafts, clothes—you name it and people send it. The support is overwhelming and puts the wind in my sails to fight another day.

### Tracy Simon

The CNN story plays several times on May 26 and 27. Hopefully the message to OPTN/UNOS is loud and clear. Phone conversations and text messages with the family at the hospital keep us up to date on Sarah's ever-changing condition. Team Sarah adds seven additional public relations professionals to the team, and we pool our collective resources and divide and conquer.

Maureen, who has worked extensively in crisis public relations, develops our overall strategy while the rest of us divide the work of focusing on the budding legal battle, beginning a political outreach campaign, drafting our first press release, and communicating clearly and regularly with the media. Something that needs to be communicated clearly—and with a solid analogy— is that Janet and Fran are not asking for preference for Sarah.

Most of the members of Team Sarah are moms with young kids, and some of us are working full-time. Keeping up with the frantic pace of the story and communicating with each other is a challenge. Sarah's story is catching fire—in today's terms, we are going viral.

I become the primary face of Sarah's story. All day long, I take my un-showered, sleep-deprived self out to the curb just off CHOP's property to do live and taped interviews. I return to snuggling my girl and making critical health care decisions, only to step back out to appear live via Skype from the hallway outside my daughter's room or take phone interviews. All day long I am interviewed, with the PR team managing the media flow and prioritizing for me. At night before bed, the team and I all come together for the next steps. Fran takes over with Sarah when I am working, and when I just can't do it anymore, he takes those interviews, too.

## Sharon

Once the media interest escalates, I do television interviews "in studio" because Janet and Fran will not go that far from Sarah, and I do interviews "on the curb" when Sarah is too sick for Janet or Fran to leave her for even a minute. I have never been interviewed on national TV before; I have no experience, yet the stakes are high, and I am constantly peppering Team Sarah for feedback to improve my ability so that I can do the best job possible for Sarah.

Thankfully, Janet is incredible on camera. She can powerfully and clearly convey the emotion and importance of the issue. One afternoon, a reporter tells Janet during an interview that OPTN's latest reason children under twelve cannot be compared to adults is that children's LAS cannot be calculated accurately and, therefore, OPTN is unable to determine how close to death a child is. When the reporter asks Janet what she would say to John Roberts, she looks straight into the camera and replies emotionally, "I invite John Roberts to come visit my daughter and tell me she is not dying."

I find I am questioning myself less. The story is gaining traction, and the UNOS arguments are weak and easily debated; they are full of false equivalences. I'm happy to be fighting. If my daughter dies, her blood will be on their hands. I'll make certain of that.

Dr. Stuart Sweet is the face of UNOS, and his interviews are often juxtaposed with mine. I realize he is toeing the party line, but it's hard not to take him personally. Somewhere deep inside me, I know that the doctors at UNOS made these rules with the best of intentions and that the results are clearly unintended consequences. I try to remind myself that these are doctors just like my Dr. Goldfarb and Dr. Panitch, but it's hard to compare. The thing that's blowing my mind is that when faced with their own data that proves my daughter is being disadvantaged, they seem more interested in saving face than in righting a wrong.

I watch their interviews with pure frustration. Think about it in the simplest terms. We have almost all been to the emergency room with an illness. In the ER, patients are treated based on how sick they are and how likely they are to die soon. This triage approach is how the lung transplant system works for everyone twelve and older. And this approach saves lives. It's logical.

But imagine a different system, one where children are put in line after all the adults and teens, regardless of how sick they are. If a child comes to this ER with major head trauma, they are not moved to the front of the line next to an adult or teen with a similar injury; they are put at the back of the line, after everyone, even those with a sprained ankle.

Specifically, kids who would benefit from twelve-and-over lung donation are put in the back of the line after all the adults and teens. In this lung transplant line, there are 2,500 adults and teens waiting. At the back of the line, there are sixty kids under twelve waiting.

We are not asking that the children get preferential treatment and go to the front of the line. We are only asking that children be in line with the adults and teens based on how sick they are.

UNOS has suggested that moving children under twelve into this line based on how sick they are will cause more teens and adults to die. There are two things wrong with this. First, we should not prioritize the life of an adult or teen over the life of a child; they should be equal. Second, treating all patients in the order of how sick they are leads to fewer people dying. UNOS's own data has proven this, and it is the reason the adults and teens are in line by order of how sick they are.

UNOS would say that the children under twelve have a separate line. A line for kids only. In the kid line, twenty lungs are handed out. In the adult/teen line, almost two thousand lungs are handed out. For many of the kids, the new lungs will work just as well whether they get the lungs from the kid line or adult line. Which line would you want your child in?

UNOS would then say that it would not be fair for the kids to get to be in both lines, because teens and adults are too big to get in the kid line. Does it make sense to deny children the chance at two thousand lungs because teens and adults don't have access to twenty additional lungs? Which is more unjust?

UNOS would say there is not enough data on children, so they cannot put the kids in with the adults. Since 2005, sixty children have died waiting in this line. How many more kids need to die for them to think they have enough data?

UNOS would say that they cannot make this work in their computer system. Even the kids in line know that all that is needed is their birthday changed in the computer system.

Dr. Sweet and I debate back and forth in the media, but I am clearly winning in the court of public opinion. The question is: Will it matter?

## Sarah

So, an amazing thing happened to me this week. I got interviewed by a famous reporter from CNN. Mom says my story was on TV and that so many people liked it that other news stations started playing it, too. I am a little bit famous, just a tiny bit, but it's pretty cool for a girl who hasn't left her hospital bed in forever.

The reporter said that she thinks I am brave. Mom says that people are inspired by my story. I could not believe it, and it makes me feel really good.

I did feel a little bad after the reporter left, because I think I was too honest about how hard it all is. The reporter cried at the end, and I think Mommy cried, too, although she tried to hide it. I told Mommy that if someone comes to interview me again, I will try to be more cheerful. Mommy says that I should always be honest even if it makes people cry. This seems like bad advice. I mean, I want them to want to come back.

Anyway, my mom also tells me that the video of me playing the xylophone and singing "Twinkle, Twinkle, Little Star" is very popular. She says people love me and are praying for me.

I have always wanted to be a famous singer, so this is very exciting. I am going to start creating more of my own original songs for Mom to record. You never know—maybe I can get them on TV, too. The next time someone comes, if that ever happens, I'm going to sing them an original piece.

# 8. Politics

A great deal happens over the next several days. The next big break comes in the form of Fox News. Peter Johnson Jr., an appellate and trial lawyer and analyst for Fox, comes down from the network's New York offices to meet Sarah, and it is clear that he is passionate about our cause. Peter also gets what it is like to be Sarah—he suffered from a life-threatening disease as a teen. For the first time since the CNN interview, I decide to allow a reporter into our room to meet Sarah, and Peter and Sarah hit it off. He adores her and she him, kindred spirits.

Peter sees the injustice for what it is and is willing to step into the fire with us. After spending the better part of the day at CHOP, he returns to New York and champions our cause. On air, Peter calls it what it is—a civil rights violation—and makes an argument for a lawsuit. This was our first thought, too.

## Maureen Garrity (Janet's friend from her public relations days)

To continue the flow of support for the Murnaghans, I come up with the idea of posting an online petition on Change.org with the hope of engaging and educating the public about transplant policy and to provide a focus for our social media activity. Based on the interest we are seeing from readers of Sarah's story, we feel giving people something they can do about the situation will help to keep them invested.

In the first four hours, five hundred people sign the petition. Within days, we were up to one hundred thousand signatures. I don't think any of us fully understood the power of the internet until we watched this petition take off. Each time someone signs, the petition pops into the inbox of Dr. John Roberts, president of OPTN/UNOS. We hear that his inbox crashes after around forty-eight thousand emails.

As Peter argues day in and day out for us, other Fox News anchors begin to fight, too. Everyone is talking about Sarah. The PR team knows we need to quantify for UNOS what the American people think of their policy in a very tangible way, so they create a Change .org petition. It explodes as well. Our family shares the petition with everyone we know. Soon, our entire community is behind us, with our local schools, Little League, and businesses sharing the petition. Quickly, we have tens of thousands of signatures, and it grows daily by leaps and bounds, eventually reaching nearly four hundred thousand.

### Allow transplants of adult lungs to children

By Family and Friends of Sarah Murnaghan

May 28, 2013

Ten-year-old Sarah Murnaghan has end-stage Cystic Fibrosis
and has been on the lung transplant list for 18 months. Too
sick to leave Children's Hospital of Philadelphia for three
months, she has only a week or two before she will lose her
battle. If she were two years older, she would have a high
probability of receiving lungs in time. Sarah is eligible for
adult donor lungs, but because of her age, she will only
receive them after all adult candidates, regardless of how
sick they are, have the opportunity to accept them.

This is a policy created by the Organ Procurement and
Transplantation Network (OPTN), the nation's organ
procurement, donation and transplantation system and
enforced through United Network for Organ Sharing (UNOS)
which manages the US organ transplant system under
contract with the federal government.

Based on a 2000 ruling by the U.S. Department of Health
and Human Services, which mandated that organ allocation
policies must be based on medical necessity rather than
waiting time, OPTN implemented a new allocation system
based on the severity of a patient's illness (the Lung
Allocation Score, or LAS), rather than the amount of time
served on the wait list in 2005. This reduced the number of
deaths among patients awaiting lung transplant, ensured
lungs were allocated to those with less stable diagnoses, and
dramatically reduced the average wait time from over two
years, and reduced the wait list by half. This new approach
only applied to patients over the age of twelve. This approach
was not extended to children. Despite the fact that many
pediatric patients can use a partial lobar transplant from an
adult donor, these young patients are only offered adult
donor lungs after all adult patients, regardless of the severity
of the child's illness. While Sarah has an LAS score over 60,
which would normally place her as the highest priority for her

blood type in the region, all adults in the region with her blood type will be offered the lungs first, even those with more stable diagnoses and lower LAS scores. Sarah will only be offered adult lungs if no adult candidates accept the organ.

Sarah is a top priority on the pediatric list, but the pediatric donors are far fewer than the adult donors, dramatically reducing the number of lungs Sarah is offered. So far in 2013, there were 1,133 adult deceased lung donors and only seventy under the age of twelve. The result is only four pediatric lung donor recipients in 2013, and 291 for those over twelve years old.

This policy needs to change. The OPTN/UNOS Lung Review Board, a national group of transplant physicians and surgeons, can make an exceptional ruling for Sarah. And they can recommend new policies to OPTN. John Roberts is President of the OPTN/UNOS Board of Directors.

This petition was delivered to:
President, Board of Directors, OPTN/UNOS
John Roberts
Secretary, Health and Human Services
Kathleen Sebelius

Our supporters are not just signing the petition; they are picking up the phone and making calls to John Roberts, the president of OPTN, and Kathleen Sebelius, the secretary of Health and Human Services under President Barack Obama. We are applying as much pressure as humanly possible.

Team Sarah is driving the narrative, constantly and conscientiously offering the media new status updates on Sarah and new angles to discuss. Our biggest challenge is finding experts outside CHOP willing to talk and drive the conversation. Twitter handles start trending #sign4sarah, #hopeforsarah, and #sarahmurnaghan, and even Katy Perry tweets about Sarah. One of Fran's colleagues, all the way in Singapore, says Sarah is making the news there, too. They are talking about Sarah across the world.

We have clearly won in the court of public opinion; people do not think Sarah is being treated fairly. But UNOS remains firm. They will do nothing and change nothing, and we are running out of time. More and more, it seems to me that they do not want to change things out of principle. I have challenged their authority, and they do not want it done that way. They want their process respected. I believe, at this point, that they know I am right; they just are unwilling to admit it.

Meanwhile, Sarah is dying. I am watching her slip away. Sarah's eyes are heavy and droopy most of the time now. She is so fragile, weak, and little, so dependent because of her severe illness. I hug and kiss her all day long. At times, Sarah has raging fevers from the infected mucus in her lungs. This is unbelievably terrifying. Every time Sarah spikes a fever, doctors run another culture on her mucus to make sure there is not a virus. A virus at this stage of the wait for transplant would be a death sentence. Viruses disqualify you from the transplant list until they have run their course, and Sarah would not live through a virus. There are so many things that could go wrong here. We don't have time for this. More and more, it seems that being right is not going to matter in the end, because UNOS is not willing to admit they are wrong.

Due to Team Sarah outreach, but to my complete surprise, Sarah's story suddenly becomes a political hot potato. I should see it coming, but I don't. Pennsylvania senator Pat Toomey and congressman Pat Meehan, a representative for Pennsylvania's Seventh Congressional District, are the first to step forward and offer us support. It happens one morning on a live shot I am doing from "the curb" at CHOP. Representative Meehan is live at the Fox studios arguing on our behalf. I have to hold back my tears of pure gratitude as I hear him calling on Kathleen Sebelius to step up and do something.

Shortly after this interview, I hear that Senator Toomey has come out publicly supporting us as well. Both Pennsylvania representatives are willing to fight on Sarah's behalf. This turns into a major breakthrough for us. Their public cries of foul add legitimacy to our fight. I am not just a crazy mom shouting at the cameras; something is wrong here.

Their next steps are critical. Both Senator Toomey and Representative Meehan reach out directly to Kathleen Sebelius. They publish public letters they have written to her. Following them, other members of the Senate and Congress step forward, not just Pennsylvania representatives but mostly Republicans. We have legitimate support—a lot of it, in fact. And finally, Secretary Sebelius's office calls and sets up a time to speak with me directly.

The call is cordial—kind, even—but at the same time totally baffling. She says sympathetic things; she talks about being a mom and a grandmother and how truly awful this situation is. She's warm and kind in a forced sort of way. But I am playing ball. I will be her personal cheerleader if that's what it takes.

Then the conversation turns. She says that she does not have the authority to do anything. Now, here's the problem: I know this is not true. Before this call, I did my research (or Sharon's lawyer friend Erin did), and I know the law, and she does, in fact, have the authority. I even know the exact section of the law that gives her the authority and exactly what authority she has. Is she that incompetent that she does not know her own authority, or is she just playing me?

I politely cite the law and the exact location in the law that she can reference that gives her the authority. I tell her she has the ability to intervene immediately for Sarah and other children on a temporary basis, as well as to instruct UNOS to immediately study the issue for a permanent change in the rule. She assures me she will look into it in detail and asks if she can call me the next day. I agree, even though I don't know if Sarah has another day of waiting left in her. Hope and faith spring eternal for me, because without them I have very little to hang on to.

I try to lie low in the media while she is making this decision; I don't want to anger her. Peter Johnson Jr. has given me this advice, saying, "If [Sebelius] is backed into a corner, she will bite." I take this advice very seriously.

Meanwhile, though, the media is more on fire with the story than ever. Conservative talk show hosts and members of the Republicans in Congress are drawing the line between Sarah's fight to live and be heard by UNOS as an example of a bureaucrat, not the child's own doctors, making life and death medical decisions—so-called death panels. The concern over death panels began as the Obama administration was rolling out the Patient Protection and Affordable Care Act, which would later be known as the Affordable Care Act (ACA) and nicknamed "Obamacare." It is the idea that a bureaucrat somewhere will decide who lives and who dies instead of the patient's doctor. Kathleen Sebelius is that bureaucrat, and while we do not personally have Obamacare, it's not hard to connect the dots and put a face to that concern, and that face becomes Sarah's.

As a longtime Democrat and proponent of Obamacare, I don't love that this is how our story is being portrayed, yet I can't deny it. It's upsetting to me that Democrats are not coming out publicly supporting us, although many support us privately. The laws that are standing in Sarah's way were actually developed during the Bush administration. Additionally, this does not feel like a Republican-versus-Democrat thing to me. A little girl is dying; that's not political.

I feel panic as each minute, hour, and day ticks by. Sarah's death gets closer and closer. It's like being stuck on train tracks with a train barreling down at you. You scream, but no one comes. I'm screaming, and the world is watching me in horror, but the person driving the train, the only person who can stop this, just sits and watches. That person is Kathleen Sebelius.

The next day arrives, May 31, 2013. Kathleen Sebelius's office asks to push back our promised call. I agree and wait with bated breath. The hour rolls by, and they ask for another extension and then another. In the end, Sebelius never calls. Eventually, she releases a public statement ordering a policy review of the age requirements, but over the long term. We issue a public statement:

> *Secretary Sebelius' decision to not exercise her very clear authority under the law to intervene and mandate a variance that would help save Sarah's life is devastating. Essentially, Sarah has been left to die.*

We have been left reeling. At a House committee hearing, Republican Lou Barletta, representative for Pennsylvania's Eleventh Congressional District, stands up in our defense and grills Sebelius.

> *Why are we going to let a little ten-year-old girl die because she is ten and not twelve? Please suspend the rules until we look at this policy [that] we all believe is flawed . . . We have the chance to save someone's life. Please, suspend the rules until we look at this policy.*

Sebelius responds on the floor by saying something we will never forget:

> *I would suggest, sir, that, again, this is an incredibly agonizing situation where someone lives and someone dies. The medical evidence and the transplant doctors who are making the rule—and have had the rule in place since 2005 making a*

*delineation between pediatric and adult lungs, because lungs*
*are different than other organs—that it's based on the survivability*
*[chances].*

Barletta counters that medical professionals think Sarah can
survive an adult lung transplant, but Sebelius will not budge.


## Fran

What can I say about Kathleen Sebelius? Well, I do not like her
very much. You decide for yourself. I did once see a list of the top
reasons why she was considered by many to be a failure at her
job, and Sarah was on the list. I still smile when I think of that
list.


## Sarah

Today a group of my nurses from 8-South come to visit me. It's
the very best thing that could have happened. I had a very rough
morning.

You see, my respiratory therapist insisted that I switch from
my regular BiPAP mask to this full facial mask for most of the
day. I hate the full facial mask. I've used it before. It makes it
impossible to talk to anyone, and it's totally uncomfortable.

On top of that, my stomach just gets worse and worse, and I
cannot get comfortable. I cried a lot today.

So, I finally get a small break from the evil mask and the best
surprise ever happens: some of my best nurses arrive. They know
all the games I like and are so good to me. Right away I start
showing them something on my Nintendo DS and the morning
just goes away.

They are always willing to play a game with me, and we pick up right where we left off. It's like I never left 8-South at all. I show them how the sticker cards are going, who's beating them, and we have a lot of fun.

The people from 8-South are the best part of this place. Ever since I left 8-South for the scary floor, they've all taken turns visiting me. It makes me feel very special.

My brothers and sister aren't allowed to visit anymore because we have to be very careful about germs now that I am so sick. The people here in this hospital and Mom, Dad, Aunt Sharon, and Aunt Lora are all I have right now, but most of the time, it is enough.

# 9. Other Hospitals

I hold Sarah in my arms, relishing every moment with her. Fran does the same. We continue to fill the days with music, painting, and crafts; a fiery game of Monopoly is still her favorite. At night, we take turns sleeping in her bed, while the other sleeps on the padded bench in her room. The person who sleeps with Sarah gets little to no sleep, but Fran and I jokingly fight over who gets the honor—neither of us wants to lose a moment of time with our girl.

"Mommy, do you know what Daddy said while he was snuggling me today?" Sarah asks sweetly with glee in her voice.

"No, what did he say?" I ask suspiciously, knowing what might be coming next.

"He said, maybe Mommy would let him sleep with me *again* tonight." She giggles uncontrollably as she sees the mock horror on my face.

"What! That sneaky Daddy is trying to take my place?" I say, pretending to be shocked. Sarah is loving it, and she is signaling Fran to come over and join in this "fight" over her.

"I got my eye on that sneaky Daddy," I say as I hold her in my arms tightly. "It's *my* turn, and I know what he is up to," I say as Fran joins us on the bed.

There's a warmth and normalcy here, despite the storm brewing around outside this hospital room. Sarah has these moments of joy and laughter intermixed with suffering and pain. She is lucid tonight, and we are thoroughly enjoying her. I hold her in my arms, kissing and hugging her. She is so sweet.

I am devastated inside, but I've grown accustomed to putting my feelings aside and making the best of this for Sarah, who is still unaware of the very real battle for her life brewing outside this hospital room. While my friends on Team Sarah manage the media (with me taking moments away from Sarah for interviews), my sisters have been finding other angles to save Sarah's life.

Earlier in the week, Dr. Stuart Sweet of UNOS mentioned another potential path for us while he was doing a media interview. He suggested that other hospitals with less severely ill patients could defer lungs to Sarah. Hopeful for any ideas, Sharon reaches out to Dr. Sweet personally to discuss this.

## Sharon

I have a long conversation with Dr. Sweet, who is very sympathetic and is trying to help Sarah behind the scenes, despite his public stance as a representative of OPTN. He explains that the normal OPTN appeal process can only be used for narrow issues such as adjusting an individual LAS score and that there is no possible review for requests such as Sarah's. He essentially agrees there is a problem. He expresses concern over the rate of children's deaths and mentions an analysis he has done and presented to his OPTN colleagues highlighting this same issue. As a pediatric lung transplant doctor, he seems to share our frustration.

He explains that lung transplant surgeons can decline a set of lungs and defer them to another surgeon's patient at a different hospital. They do this in urgent cases. If I can convince other lung transplant doctors to defer lungs to Sarah, we could save her without a change in the OPTN rules. Armed with this intelligence, I start making calls.

We call the two lung transplant centers in Philadelphia, the ones most likely to be able to defer lungs directly to her. Temple University's head of transplant is the first to agree, without equivocation. Sarah's LAS is higher than all his patients, and he agrees that the sickest should get lungs. University of Pennsylvania is sympathetic but noncommittal, offering to discuss it further internally. They later refuse, the only to do so and the most important.

This is my first opportunity to speak with a wide range of lung transplant doctors. Surprisingly, most agree that the under-twelve rule is arbitrary and that, given the ability to section lungs, should not be in place. I can't help but ask why the rule is still in place. Many describe an OPTN board that is slow to move and unable to make decisions.

After dozens of calls, most centers agree to defer lungs to Sarah if she has the higher LAS score. Some need to take it to a board vote and will do so immediately. OPTN will need to follow up with them, but I have the list of centers that are supportive, including Duke University, Cleveland Clinic, University of Pittsburgh, New York–Presbyterian/Columbia University Medical Center, Indiana University of Health, Tampa General Hospital, Emory University, Brigham and Women's Hospital, University of Maryland, and Inova.

With this success, I call the Gift of Life, the local UNOS center, on the next steps.

Sarah is by far the sickest—the only one with a potential to die—in the Philadelphia region. Her LAS score proves this. Lora and Sharon spearhead this process tracking down the email addresses and phone numbers for the heads of the lung transplant programs regionally and throughout the country. Lora later tells me that it was hard to even get through switchboards and speak directly with the critical people but that Sharon was shameless and would somehow get the right stakeholders on the phone eventually, whether they wanted to be gotten hold of or not.

It's not clear to us exactly who can defer lungs to Sarah. We know the local programs are at the top of the list, so we start there and work our way through. The head of the Temple program is supportive, agreeing that Sarah is, without a doubt, the sickest person in the region and, therefore, should be at the top of the list. He immediately agrees to defer an offer of adult lungs to Sarah as long as he does not have a patient with a higher LAS when the offer is made.

Excited by this initial success, we move on to the University of Pennsylvania. We know that for Temple's offer to work, the University of Pennsylvania must also agree to the plan; otherwise, any deferral of lungs from Temple will not go to Sarah but to the next adult on the list in Philadelphia, most likely a Penn patient. Luckily, Penn and CHOP are partner programs, so we assume that since Temple has agreed, we are in the home stretch, but within hours, we are devastated to be told no by Penn—despite their knowing that Sarah is sicker than any of their patients by far.

Months later, I learn that UNOS was also petitioning Penn to help Sarah; they, too, wanted Penn to defer lungs to her, since they did not have a critically ill patient, but Penn also told them no. At the time, I feel bitter toward Penn and vow Sarah will never be an adult patient there. But in hindsight, this begs the question: Why wouldn't UNOS do it themselves, officially in their system, if they believed Penn should do it?

While making these calls, we have two other things we are looking for. First, is there another hospital willing to dual list Sarah? This is critical, because if we are unable to work the system and have lungs deferred to Sarah as UNOS has recommended, maybe we can bring Sarah to the organ by listing her at a different hospital. This is an allowed and accepted practice in transplant medicine. But it also begs the question: Why make the critically ill patient travel when you can more safely move the organ? The deeper I dig, the more concerns and questions I come up with.

Unfortunately, centers almost uniformly agree that Sarah is too ill to be transferred. We are not just speaking to pediatric centers; we also are asking adult centers if they would consider listing Sarah. We finally find one pediatric center willing to consider a dual list and transfer if an organ becomes available—Nationwide Children's Hospital in Ohio—and we begin the process of providing them with background information on Sarah to see if this is a viable option. All the adult centers, while feeling capable of transplanting her, uniformly agree that their licensing will not allow them to transplant a child under fifteen or sixteen years of age.

The second question we have surrounds live donor transplants. CHOP does not do live lung donor transplants because they believe the risk to the healthy donor is too high. It's not like a kidney donation. Despite this, the adults in our family are ready and willing to accept that risk, and so we press on. We find there is no pediatric program willing to do a live donor lung transplant. We do find that Duke, an adult center, is willing to do live donor lung transplants in extreme circumstances, but since Sarah is ten years old, they cannot operate on her, so the live donor option is off the table.

We find in talking off the record with other pediatric lung transplant programs that they almost universally say they agree with our fight for Sarah. They agree that children like her are at a disadvantage; they see it in their own patients. They are losing patients at a much greater rate due to a lack of access to donor lungs. They are quietly cheering us on. Even the one director of a large pediatric program who yells at Sharon for "dragging Dr. Sweet and UNOS through the mud" concedes there is a real issue.

We try to get one of these doctors—who believe children are being hurt by the current system—to speak out, but they refuse. Their licensing to do transplants is regulated by UNOS, and several say they fear retribution if they come out publicly. We do not know if this is a real or imagined risk, but it is keeping them silent.

Sharon's next step is to call the local Organ Procurement Organization (OPO), which is charged with matching donors and recipients to coordinate the implementation of the plan for cooperating transplant centers to defer lungs to Sarah. Armed with a long list of these centers—and believing we are following the direction and advice of a UNOS representative—she is unprepared for the hostility she receives from the OPO, whose staff berates her and accuses us of trying to steal lungs.

With hours and hours of calls logged and time quickly running out, each of these blows tears us apart. My sweet, precious girl is slipping away. Many lung transplant doctors across the United States have agreed to help; Dr. Sweet has suggested we pursue them, yet we are accused of heinous things by our local OPO. Meanwhile, politicians stand up both publicly and quietly, saying we are right, only to be told by Secretary Sebelius, "Someone must live and someone must die." Her ruling stands with the Obama White House, I suppose, but I don't understand how this could be. I keep waiting for someone to overrule her, but it doesn't happen.

Years later, while watching the movie *Sully*, Sharon and I will equate the injustice we feel at this moment to that of Captain Sully Sullenberger (Chesley Burnett Sullenberger III). If you haven't seen the movie, Sully was seen by the public and the media as heroic for making critical last-minute decisions that saved the lives of all 155 passengers aboard Flight 1549, which he was piloting when it was disabled by a flock of Canadian geese shortly after takeoff on January 15, 2009. Sully managed to make an emergency landing in the Hudson River off Manhattan. But after the incident, he found himself vilified by the Federal Aviation Administration (FAA), which seemed intent on scapegoating him as the villain rather than the hero.

Like Captain Sully, we are doing the best we can to save Sarah's life and the lives of those in similar circumstances. There are real children dying. And while the media and the public see our fight as heroic, we feel villainized by authorities behind the scene, who seem focused on discrediting us and making it look like we are the problem, not those who continue to allow children to die under the existing system. It is hard to swallow these attacks.

When I started this fight just a week ago, I felt alone, overwhelmed, and paralyzed. It was hard to see a way forward. I had to physically will myself out of bed each morning. But a lot has changed in a week, and I have changed, too. I am still scared out of my mind, terrified that I will lose Sarah, but my rage at the injustice is now the overwhelming driving force, fueling me like adrenaline. The more I am accused of being the villain while children die under an inequitable federal system, the more determined I become to fight. I am going to fight until Sarah's last breath—pray to God it never comes to that—and then I will go on to fight for the next child. This is not over.

### Sarah

There's a new building being built just outside our window. When Mom and I arrived in February, they were digging a hole in the ground and framing the underground garage. I would sit by the window in my room on 8-South and watch the men with cranes. It was amazing to see a whole building go up right before my eyes. Hundreds, maybe thousands, of people taking part in it. Mom and I would just sit and watch.

Now, in June, I am sitting in the PICU, but my view is almost exactly the same, just from a different height. I think I am on the sixth floor now. The whole building looks mostly framed to me. It must be at least ten stories high. It's crazy to think that just a few months ago it was just a hole in the ground. Mom says it's nowhere near being ready because they have to do the inside, too, but I can't help thinking I have been in the hospital so long that workers have been able to build a ten-story building.

When will this ever end? Will I ever get to go home and be with my family again? Will I ever get to take that first big breath with my new lungs? This wait seems never-ending.

# 10. The Lawsuit

Sarah feels like life is passing her by. It is tremendously hard to watch all your friends graduate from elementary school while you are still stuck in the hospital unable to even attend. It is tremendously hard to watch your siblings revel in the excitement of the start of the summer and the pool season while you struggle to get out of bed. Sarah is just ten years old, and all she dreams of is to be a typical kid playing outside and going to school. At times these dreams seem unattainable to us, yet so easy for everyone else. We don't begrudge anyone else these experiences. We just want them, too.

Some days Sarah cries and immerses herself in sadness. I cry, too. I feel so angry. She is being cheated out of her childhood. It feels very unfair. It is hard to pull yourself out of this feeling, but it is also no way to live. So today we actively try to focus on the good memories—all the things Sarah has gained rather than lost over the past few months. They say happiness is a choice. I'm not sure that's always true, but we certainly try to choose happiness as much as we can.

Right now, hanging in Sarah's hospital room is a long paper

chain. Each link represents one day at CHOP, and Sarah has written a good memory from each day on each link of the chain. Sarah made this amazing chain spanning over one hundred days at CHOP with her child-life specialist Kate. Sarah calls her Big-Bun Kate because she often wears her hair in a big bun, and when Sarah asks for her, she does not want you to get confused and bring the wrong Kate (one of the Kates is a physical therapist, and Sarah does not love to do physical therapy). Kate does crafts that I could never dream up—I don't know where she comes up with these ideas—and helps Sarah manage all her feelings and experiences.

### Sarah

This chain that Big-Bun Kate and I made is special to me. It represents all that I have been through. Looking back at some of my best times helps remind me that it hasn't been all bad. Mom and I curl up on my bed and drape my giant paper chain across our laps. On some days I've written nothing—I guess I didn't have anything nice to say those days—but there are a lot of good memories here, too.

On day forty-nine, I wrote: "Cake pop day! Today I made cake pops with Chef Barry!" This was one of my favorite days at CHOP. Big-Bun Kate planned for Chef Barry to come to my room and make cake pops with me. This was a very special event; none of the other kids on the hallway were getting to do this. Kate says it's the good part of being in the hospital for so long—sometimes you get extra special treats that no one else gets. This day made me feel like a kid, doing normal stuff again. My favorite part was decorating the cake pops with sprinkles and then sharing them with my favorite nurses and doctors.

On day fifty-one, I wrote: "Oreo puddin' Murnaghan visits!"

Oreo is my dog; Puddin' is a middle name I made up for him. For a long, long time, I told the doctors over and over again about how much I missed my dog, Oreo. It sucked that he could not visit me. After all, he is part of the family, too, I would tell them, and you know what? They all agreed. Then one day, after what seemed like the longest wait to get my dog approved by the hospital, Oreo was finally allowed to visit. I was very excited when he came with Uncle Bunky. Uncle Bunky might actually love Oreo as much as I do. Anyway, as excited as I was to see Oreo, I think he was even happier to see me and all the new people. He really loved it, but thankfully he did not pee with excitement—that's something he does sometimes. He was a good boy. He didn't even bark and annoy everyone; he pretty much snuggled with me on my bed and tried to steal my food. I put Cheerios on the bed for him to eat and bounced the bed so the Cheerios would pop up and down. He liked this game, catching them in his mouth. After this day, Oreo kept coming, and the days that he came were always some of my favorites.

On day seventy-five, I wrote: "Sean, Finn, and Ella came to visit. Aunt Sharon stocked me up with a bunch of new toys." Aunt Sharon would always go to the toy store and get me two whole bags of toys, including board games, crafts, and just about anything that would help me pass the time. Obviously, I love this. A lot of times when she came to visit, she would bring my siblings, too. When I was healthier, they would come as a big group, maybe once a week, and then one at a time, maybe once or twice a week also, depending on how I was doing. Right now, though, I can't see them anymore. The last time I saw everyone was for my PICU send-off party. Anyway, when they would come as a group, I would get very excited. We would all pile into the bed and use the controls to lift the bed as high as it would go. Then we usually played a board game, did a craft, and just talked. If I was tired, we would snuggle and watch a movie.

It wasn't always easy, though. Sometimes Sean would get very emotional after a while and start crying; he's only in first grade and really misses us. Finn would do OK; he doesn't really understand what is going on, so I think that makes it easier. Ella understands, and she's sad, too, but she was usually quiet about it. She only cried one time when she did not want to leave. One of our best times was when everyone came to celebrate Ella's birthday. They brought a cake, and we partied just like we would have if we were at home.

Just a couple of days ago, on day one hundred, I wrote: "We had a party with bubbles, music, and a sign! After I was in the hospital for one hundred days!" This was a very special day. Everyone knows it's hard to be here, so having my one hundredth–day celebration felt good. It really is a major accomplishment. Kate brought a big bubble machine; there were bubbles everywhere. She made a big sign that is still hanging in my room, and we played music. Bubbles are my thing! Mom and Dad were on the bed with me, and we were blowing bubbles everywhere. I think we blew bubbles until we ran out and the floor was a slippery, soapy mess. I even had a bubble gun that lit up.

I really want to go home now. I am done with all of this. I don't want to be waiting in the hospital forever, because that's what it feels like to me. It feels like in ten years I will still be here waiting.

I want Sarah to walk out of this hospital someday and get the chance to be a kid again. We have been here for months, but even before that, for the past eighteen months, she was tethered to an oxygen tank, confined mostly to our house, with just short trips out. That wasn't really living either. After all this waiting and suffering, all this hope and prayer, I cannot accept that she will die. It's just so terribly unfair.

Our next step is obvious. We have exhausted all the other options, and now it is time to take our case to the courts.

## Sharon

I contact all the major law firms in Philadelphia to ask for pro bono support for Sarah. Most firms demur, either due to existing representation of CHOP or Gift of Life or because the likelihood of winning is low. One firm comes back and offers to take the case—Pepper Hamilton and its partner Steve Harvey.

The escalating media coverage, especially with Peter Johnson Jr. laying out the legal basis for fighting this injustice, turns the tide in our favor, as well as Janet's friend Anne Bongiovanni working her own personal legal contacts at Steve's firm. And now, at this critical moment, we have arguably the largest, most respected law firm in Philadelphia representing us.

As I detail the case to Steve, he is sympathetic, but it is clear he views the case as a long shot. Then I outline the numbers. Kids are dying at twice the rate of adults, based on UNOS's own data. Steve is skeptical, and I can't blame him. It seems highly unlikely something like this would be allowed to happen. He contacts his statistician, and two hours later, the statistician confirms my findings—children under twelve are dying at twice the rate of those over twelve.

Steve is a person with a strong sense of right and wrong and a passion to fight injustice. At this point, he becomes relentless. We spend the next eight hours discussing Sarah's case in detail: the stats and the history of UNOS. Steve cancels his plans for the evening and lays out the legal strategy. He will argue a civil rights violation, based on age discrimination, and seek a temporary injunction.

Later that day, I finally return to the hospital, when Janet calls to say Sarah has taken a turn for the worse.

As the weekend wears on, Sarah's status declines. Will we make it? I just don't know. I call Sharon to tell her she should come back. This might be it. Lora sits quietly on the bench in Sarah's room; Fran is by my side, quiet. We are together in this room but distant. We are each surviving in our own way, and taking on each other's emotions as well is more than either of us can bear, so we sit quietly in our own private pain. I will no longer leave to speak to the media and do the updates, so Fran takes over.

Sarah's fevers are raging again. When I touch her, she is burning up. As she shakes, I pick her up, along with her tangled mess of wires, and hold her in my arms just rocking her back and forth in the hard, wooden hospital rocking chair. She looks so tiny and helpless. As a mother, you are supposed to protect your children from harm; I can't do that. I am failing her. All I can do is hold her and try to comfort her as she suffers painfully. As I rock her in the chair, I am stroking her hair, trying to provide even the tiniest bit of comfort. She shakes uncontrollably, even while sleeping, for what feels like hours. As the fever finally abates, I wrap her in a soft blanket and just stare down at her. I wish I could freeze this moment, because the next will surely be worse. I can't make her better, but I will not let her go!

# 11. Our Day in Court

Ten days ago, we began the public fight to save Sarah's life, and today seems like the culmination of that effort. Sharon and Steve left for court first thing this morning to file a temporary restraining order (TRO) to stop Secretary Sebelius from barring Sarah access to the organs she so desperately needs. This is our last hope. If we can't win here, surely, we have lost Sarah forever.

It's beyond frustrating. The laws standing between life and death for Sarah are arbitrary. What scientific data was used to determine twelve was the cutoff for being triaged, for having access to thousands of organs versus a few handfuls? Why not eleven years old? Why not ten years old? What is it about Sarah as a ten-year-old dying from CF that is so different from a twelve-year-old dying with CF? I will tell you—*nothing*. Yet because of this age difference, Sarah will likely die.

## Sharon

I meet Steve at the courthouse to file the emergency injunction in court. Within an hour of filing, we are called in for our case. The Department of Justice is representing the government's position, and given the short timing, the main lawyer is on a conference call. Two additional lawyers from the Justice Department sit at the opposing council table and barely speak during the hearing.

Michael Baylson, USDJ, senior U.S. district judge for the Eastern District of Pennsylvania, has clearly read Steve's brief in advance and after just a few questions wants to hear from Sarah's doctor. It is clear Sarah's doctor is critical to his decision. He adjourns while we wait for Dr. Goldfarb.

As we are sitting in the hall waiting, the anticipation is killing me. I have no idea how the case will look through the judge's eyes, and I am extremely anxious. Everything is riding on this. It is clear from our brief time in the courtroom that Dr. Goldfarb's testimony will be the lynchpin, but I have no idea what he will say; he has not been prepped.

Dr. Goldfarb arrives about an hour later. He sits casually, juxtaposed to the sea of ties, suits, and stiff collars that make up the legal teams. I am sitting anxiously on the edge of my seat as he takes the stand. He seems calm and relaxed, unfazed. The opposite of how I feel.

The judge gets right to the point in questioning Dr. Goldfarb. Would Sarah live as long as an adult post-transplant? Yes, longer. Would her quality of life be good? Yes, she could grow up, go to college, and get married. Would adult lungs work on Sarah? Yes, just as well as on an adult.

The judge's body language is changing now. He is confused by the under-twelve rule, and I can feel the momentum changing in the room.

Is there a medical difference between those under and over twelve? No, says Goldfarb. Then why the under-twelve rule? Dr. Goldfarb says it is medically arbitrary. They needed a cutoff for distributing pediatric lungs and picked twelve.

*Arbitrary.* The most beautiful word in the English language to me right now. In the last few days, I have become familiar with the legal language on civil rights violations. One of the key factors for determining if a rule is discriminatory is whether it is arbitrary. My hopes soar on *arbitrary.* The judge's demeanor changes. He has moved from trying to determine the reason for the rule to realizing there is not one. He realizes this is an injustice.

The Justice Department lawyer realizes the judge is about to rule against them. She argues that it isn't under the judge's purview to overrule the OPTN. She argues that the OPTN is calling an emergency meeting for Monday to consider making an exception for Sarah. She suggests they probably will make an exception for Sarah and that it would be better if the OPTN makes this decision than if a judge does.

Now, I know Sarah could lose her fight between Wednesday and Monday while waiting for a conference call of the OPTN board members. In fact, I can just imagine an assistant scheduling that OPTN call and moving it to accommodate the OPTN board executives' schedules. Disgusting. That group of doctors knows more than anyone that Sarah could die in those four days. The complete disregard for one child's life stuns me. And the judge clearly shares my disgust and shock. He is emphatic that he will not withhold justice for four days to allow the OPTN to make the same decision knowing Sarah could die in those four days. And in that moment, Sarah's life is saved.

Back in the hospital, we are ecstatic when we receive the news that the judge has granted the TRO. This is no guarantee that Sarah will get a match in time, but it requires Secretary Sebelius to place her in the donor pool based on illness, not age, for the next ten days until the judge can hear the case. The relief is palpable. We release a public statement:

> *For us, this means that for the next 10 days, Sarah's placement in the queue for adult lungs will be based on the severity of her illness, and she will not be penalized for her age. (Her current LAS score— the measure used to measure illness—is a 78.)*
>
> *We are experiencing many emotions: relief, happiness, gratitude and, for the first time in months: hope.*
>
> *We cannot say enough about the global outreach and support we've received on behalf of Sarah—people of all ages and walks of life have reached out to us, prayed for us, and asked how they could help. All we can ask is that everyone TODAY takes steps to become an organ donor. The Gift of Life honors the extreme generosity of the donors and their families, and allows some of that generous spirit to live on. You can register yourself and your family immediately to become organ donors here: http://www.organdonor.gov/becomingdonor/index .html*
>
> *Thank you and God Bless.*

The judge gives the Department of Justice until 11:00 that night to list Sarah as a competing candidate twelve and over. He also tells Steve Harvey that if there is another child in this region, in a similar circumstance, he would likely rule in that child's favor, too, if Steve brought him the case.

The next day, Secretary Sebelius also releases a statement:

> *"I understand that in compliance with the Judge's order, last night at 10:34 p.m. eastern time, OPTN created a second*

*candidate record for Miss Murnaghan with a birthdate that*
*makes the system treat her as a 12-year-old. I also understand*
*that her original record remains active, so she retains her priority*
*for pediatric donors," Sebelius said. "I appreciate your immediate*
*attention to the court's order."*

We are national news and for the first time feel a public on-
slaught of ethics folks speaking publicly on behalf of the federal
government. A few ethics experts take issue with us bringing the
case to court, saying this is not how the system should work. This
blows my mind, as this is exactly how the system of checks and
balances in the United States is supposed to work. Following the
ruling, the judge releases an explanation:

*The Court explained in some detail its reasons for issuing the*
*Temporary Restraining Order ("TRO") during the hearing on*
*June 5, 2013. This case has been widely reported in the media.*
*Some of the public commentary reveals that the individuals*
*making comments have not listened to the audio transcript of the*
*hearing where the Court detailed its reasoning for issuing the*
*Order. Two of the important reasons are as follows:*
*First, Dr. Goldfarb, the physician for Plaintiffs' daughter,*
*Sarah, and an expert in the field of pediatric pulmonology,*
*testified that the "Under 12 Rule" was developed almost 9 years*
*ago and that, based on the medical and scientific experience that*
*has accrued since that time, he believes the rule is "arbitrary," at*
*least as applied to children between the ages of 5 and 11 who, like*
*Sarah, have a disease process that is found in adults. Dr. Goldfarb*
*testified that children in this group can now successfully receive*
*adult lungs (often via a surgery that reduces the size of the lung),*
*with survival rates and long-term outcomes that are essentially the*
*same as adults.*

*A second factor underlying the Court's ruling was the government's appropriate disclosure at the hearing that the Organ Procurement and Transplantation Network ("OPTN")— the national board that administers the organ transplant program—has scheduled an emergency meeting for Monday, June 10, 2013. One of the items on OPTN's agenda is whether it should suspend operation of the Under 12 Rule pending more detailed study. The fact that the OPTN is holding an emergency meeting for this purpose suggests, in accord with Dr. Goldfarb's testimony, that legitimate questions exist about the validity and wisdom of the Under 12 Policy.*

*Considering these and other factors, the Court concluded that issuance of the TRO was very much in the interest of the public as well as the Plaintiffs and Sarah. If, for example, the OPTN decides to suspend the rule on Monday, it would be a tragedy if Sarah were to die prior to the meeting from remaining ineligible for lungs that would have otherwise become available if she were treated as an adult.*

*Finally, this Court did not in any way, shape, or form dictate when or whether Sarah should receive a lung transplant. The only legal effect of the ruling is that, for the limited duration of the TRO, Sarah will be treated the same as adults and will receive a ranking based on the details of her case relative to others, as provided by federal statutes and regulations.*

What follows this moment of euphoria is a blur. Sarah is groggy and confused. She's barely coherent at this point. Sarah has moments of panic, where she feels she is not getting enough air. Her $CO_2$ levels are dangerously high. It's clear we have just days— maybe hours—until she is intubated and sedated, until perpetual sleep takes over. I fear every conversation will be my last. I know we are at the end.

We try to explain, in the simplest terms, what's going on in the world, that today's ruling brings her closer to lungs, but she doesn't truly grasp it. Years later, she will not remember this time period or any conversations. Despite her overall confusion, she cheers our victory with excitement, and we send the video out for the world to see, but there is not true understanding there for Sarah. There is not a true celebration, just a dim hope that maybe something good has happened that will inch her forward to a better life. Our joy and excitement are overshadowed by fear and the approaching knowledge that it may be too late to save Sarah.

# 12. Intubation and Sedation

It's the beginning of the end. Doctors explain that, to preserve Sarah's brain health and ultimately her life, they must intubate and sedate her today. It's only been a few short days since winning in court, but we have seen this coming for a while now. They also explain that, given her low lung function, intubating Sarah will be dangerous and could be fatal but that they have an excellent team in place.

I curl up in bed with Sarah as Fran sits by her side holding her hand. She is alert and hopeful, smiling this morning and trying to talk her daddy into all sorts of presents and promises. Sarah certainly knows how to seize the moment. I am holding on to every moment so tightly, hanging on her every word. I love everything about this sweet, spunky, determined kid, and I fear these are our last moments with her. Will I hear her sweet voice again? Is this the last time she will hug and kiss me? Fear is tearing me up on the inside as I smile at my precious girl and our trusting conversation.

"Sarah, Mommy and Daddy just talked to the doctors, and they plan to give you some sleepy medicine, just like you take before surgeries, but this time it would not be for a surgery but to let you rest comfortably until your lungs arrive."

"Why, Mommy?" she asks in her sweet, innocent voice.

"Your lungs are just not getting enough oxygen, honey. The doctors want to place a tube down your throat to deliver oxygen directly to your lungs. But that would feel bad if you were awake, and nobody wants you to feel bad," I explain.

"Everything is going to be OK, Sarah. When you wake up, you will have new lungs and be able to breathe just like you've always dreamed," Fran explains confidently. I am so relieved for his strength right now.

"I'm scared!"

"I know, Sarah, but Mommy and Daddy will not leave your side for one minute; we will not let anything bad happen to you. I promise," I say as I hug her tightly to me.

"Sarah, when you wake up, you will have your new lungs. That's pretty exciting," Fran says. "You just need to sleep until then. I will be right here."

It's hard to say these things without crying. We are terrified, too!

When we are finished talking, we step into the hall and let the team that is gathering know that we are ready. While the team outside is huge, just two doctors will come in at first and begin to push the sedation through her port. In everything they do here, they are loving and gentle, intentionally treating the whole child; no one else wants her frightened either.

They slowly push sedation meds through her port as we hug and hold her. She seems calm and relaxed and places her trust in Fran and me to make these critical decisions. We cannot and will not let her down. We hold her as she drifts off to sleep. Once she is clearly sedated, the team descends on our room and the work seems fast and furious. The team at CHOP is enormous, and there are probably ten to fifteen people in the room. They know the sedation itself will suppress her otherwise compromised breathing, so they want that intubation tube in as quickly as possible.

This team knows us well, and the doctors tell us that we can stay in the room if we are comfortable and won't cause a distraction. Fran leaves. It is too painful for him to watch, but I still cannot leave. No matter how hard or how ugly things get, I feel she is safest when I am there in any way, which I know right now is irrational, but this is my truth. I watch anxiously, quietly, from the corner of the room as a doctor inserts a breathing tube down Sarah's throat.

I stand there with Sharon by my side and watch as they move rapidly. We closely watch the monitors that track her oxygen levels, blood pressure, and heart rate. We have been told that a sudden drop in one stat combined with a dramatic rise in another will signal serious complications. Our eyes dart between Sarah and the monitor, and what is likely a few-minutes-long procedure feels like an eternity.

The doctors have decided that they want more access to her veins, so once the breathing tube is clearly in place and they have breath sounds and taken an X-ray, they begin to insert a PICC line in her thigh, too. All the while I sit quietly praying inside, just begging God, *Let her survive this. Stay with us, please don't leave.*

It takes a long time for the team to feel she is stable enough for them to leave the room, and Fran and I are back together with our precious girl but this time in silence. There's no sweet voice or loving embrace, and I realize as much as we have been caring for Sarah and keeping her spirits high, she has been doing the same for us. And now, without her voice, I feel like I will collapse from the fear and terror. I want her back!

## Fran

One step forward, two steps back. We won the battle in court but clearly not the war. Finally, we are on a fair field of battle, but the fight is about to get a bit fiercer. Soldiers often find it difficult to explain what they have experienced in battle. Only the band of brothers and sisters who have once been there on a battlefield seem to be able to get it. And I think that makes sense. How could someone adequately explain what these horrible experiences have been like?

The team begins to explain that it is time for Sarah to be sedated and intubated. This moves us into a whole new world. This may be the last day we get to speak to Sarah, forever. Once she is sedated and intubated, a whole new clock starts. I know Sarah cannot live in an induced coma for months or years until lungs become available. In her situation, getting more than a week or two would be very generous.

Doctors explain it all, but I already get it because I have read all that I need to read about our current situation. There is no other choice at this moment but to sedate and intubate.

Talking to the doctors in the hall was the easy part. Now I must go back into the room and explain it all to Sarah. Nothing could prepare me for explaining this all to Sarah. She is very nervous, and we try to distract her with more positive conversation.

Sharon is very helpful with this. She moves right into the "What does Sarah want when she wakes up with new lungs?" topic.

Sharon: "What do you want Daddy to get you when you wake up?"

Apparently, I am in the position to promise her anything she wants. I am slightly concerned she will ask for a horse—and for good reason. She had been taking horse riding lessons before going on oxygen.

Sarah has come to know that Daddy is a softy when it comes to his princess. Years ago, when Sarah had to get a semipermanent gastrostomy tube (G-tube), she asked for a guinea pig. She got a G-tube and a guinea pig. When Sarah had to get a semi-permanent port in her arm, she asked for a puppy. She got a puppy. As a side note, I am not a fan of dogs. So, here we are, and I am well aware that she can ask for the "big one."

Sarah starts dictating a long list of this and that while Sharon takes notes. Sharon even asks Sarah if she would like a horse. Sarah declines the horse and continues with the long list of other stuff. In all the horror I am experiencing today, this is one bullet dodged.

In between all this talk, Janet and I take turns snuggling Sarah, knowing it may be our last chance. When it is time, we stay with her until she is completely asleep. Then they come in and intubate her, and our new clock of horror starts ticking.

While I expect these moments to be calm, even boring, they are anything but. Sarah's high blood pressure and elevated heart rate seem odd to me in a fully sedated child. I have seen Sarah fully sedated and comfortable, and this is not what it looks like. I fear there is some awareness, some wakefulness, under the closed eyes, and I ask to see the doctors. But the nurse does not see what I see, so I have to insist.

The fellow who arrives agrees with me. Sarah's numbers are not that of a comfortably sedated child. He increases the sedation and pushes through a bolus. Initially, this works, and I calm and relax a little, sitting at the edge of the bed in constant view of the monitors. But after another hour, the numbers begin to rise and again the nurse and I disagree, which seems crazy to me since this is the same circumstance which led the doctor to increase her sedation earlier.

"She is on extremely high levels of sedation," she insists.

"Yes, but that hardly matters if she is not fully sedated. This is a kid who has had an unusual amount of exposure to sedation throughout her life and routinely requires more than you would expect." I am annoyed, and my voice is angry and combative.

The doctors have told me that they are forcing tremendous pressures into her lungs. It's not just a tube down her throat. These pressures would make you feel like you were choking, gasping for air. It's not a natural state at all, and it is critical that she be fully sedated. I am terrified that she will wake.

Another alarming thing is that there are thick globs of mucus foaming from her mouth, pouring out around her tube.

And then my worst nightmare happens: Sarah opens her eyes, wide and terrified, totally aware. Her face is red and puffy with panic; her eyes are bulging out of their sockets; she thinks she cannot breathe. She pulls and grasps at her tube as I try to calm her, but the overwhelming panic due to the lack of breath is something no words of reassurance can overcome. Doctors run in and push sedation into her veins, and she goes back out immediately. The doctor is clearly angry with the nurse, and they step into the hall. Why wasn't he called sooner? He wants to know if there is any sign that she is waking.

My trust in the nursing staff is shaken, and I realize that when your child is sedated and unable to speak and fight for herself, you need to be more aware, more present. Fran and I are the only voice she has. Coincidentally (or not), a new nurse shifts onto Sarah's care. She is sweet and gentle, talking to Sarah as she makes any move, watching her sedation and reacting quickly, but I am unnerved and challenging to deal with. I cannot erase the image of Sarah panicking from my mind, and I never will be able to.

After this, Fran and I agree that one of us will need to be awake always to be her voice. He suggests that he should go sleep now (the hospital provides a room), and I should sleep at night. This way Sarah will have someone by her side 24–7. This will be our pattern until Sarah wakes again—I refuse to imagine that she will not wake again. But I know when I sleep at night, it will be right here in this room, ready to jump, ready to be here for her. Even in sedation, I will not let her be without me.

Lora and Sharon become almost permanent fixtures in Sarah's room during the day, supporting me. We don't know what she can hear, so we take turns talking to her and reading to her. Lora reads her *Mrs. Piggle-Wiggle* books, which cheers up even me from time to time as I neurotically stare at the monitors and hold Sarah's hand.

As the first twenty-four hours pass, things seem to stabilize. They have found the correct amount of sedation to keep Sarah from waking, and I feel the tense muscles in my neck start to relax a little. At times, I even let go of her hand and sit on the bench in the room while one of my sisters is talking to her. But then she begins to have raging high fevers again. The doctors are clearly very concerned, and I start to fear our two-week ability to wait for donor lungs is actually much shorter than that.

They bring in a cooling mat to put under Sarah. It is soft and water-filled, attached to a machine that regulates the temperature, and I am assured that I can relax, that this will bring down the fever. In a rare moment, my sisters and I sit on the bench and have a peaceful conversation for once, distracted by the respite from our torment. About fifteen minutes pass, and I turn to hold Sarah's hand and she is a freezing icicle. The cooling mat has turned to ice and she is bluish at her extremities. I feel panic and rage. I have had it and do not mince words when I tell them what I think. Clearly, it was not in Sarah's best interest to bring her fever down that quickly and powerfully. I feel if I pause for one moment, something will happen and she will be lost to me forever.

Truth be told, we have had 99 percent tremendous nursing care, and even though we know these are only a couple of experiences out of thousands, they are tainting the way I am dealing with the nursing staff. I feel they need to prove they are trustworthy now, and the problem is that in this huge department, the nursing staff changes over frequently and just as we get comfortable, we get a new nurse that we have little or no experience with. I feel like I am going to have a nervous breakdown, and I am no longer an easy-to-deal-with mom.

In the middle of this terror, the story outside continues. The media is still lining the streets outside the hospital. I wonder, *Are they waiting for her to get a transplant or die?* It's a horrible thought. I know they would like to hear from me, but I cannot and will not leave her anymore. Sharon and Fran take on the interviews and responsibilities. While we know the battle for access to adult lungs is largely over for Sarah, the law remains in effect for other kids. Furthermore, Sarah has people who have prayed for her and loved us and cheered us on, and we owe it to them to allow them to see this through with us.

The OPTN holds the emergency meeting they had discussed in front of the judge and decides to create a temporary rule that they will study for the next year. The temporary rule will allow all children under twelve to be considered for listing on the twelve-and-over list if their doctor deems it appropriate. I am so thrilled that no other family will live through what we have lived through, but more than anything, I wonder why it took all of this for the right thing to have been done.

I said in a statement on Facebook:

> *We consider this a tremendous win for Sarah and all kids*
> *waiting for lungs. I hope Sarah's story moves people to become*

*organ donors, because more than any ruling it is the heroes who donate their organs that save lives.*

Don Hayes, MD, MS, MEd, the medical director of the lung transplant program at Nationwide Children's Hospital in Ohio, flies in to meet with us and examine Sarah. We are extremely grateful; all the other pediatric programs believe Sarah is too sick to safely transport, and they will not even consider taking us as a dual list, while Dr. Hayes takes the time to come examine her himself. It's clear from the start that he is running an aggressive program, like CHOP, and does not quickly or easily give up on patients. He explains that Sarah is not stable enough to transport intubated and sedated with the fluctuation in pressures in flight. She will need to be put on ECMO before flight.

Additionally, he sees Sarah's situation differently from the way CHOP does and is very concerned about her heart. CHOP has always reassured us that the pulmonary hypertension would vanish with new lungs, but this doctor believes we should explore the option of a heart/lung transplant. This terrifies me.

My fears with this plan are many. First, a heart/lung match is extremely hard to come by, and we are having a terrible time getting a lung match. He assures us that his region is not as difficult in terms of access, which is an interesting thing I had noticed through my research, too. His stats support this claim. The second reason this terrifies me is that the long-term outcomes are much riskier with the heart/lung combo. So, it's harder to get a match, and the post-transplant outcomes tend to be worse. This is the only way he feels comfortable taking Sarah.

He leaves us to think it through, but I am pretty rattled by his visit. Is Sarah's heart much worse than CHOP is letting on? A new panic returns, and I quiz Dr. Goldfarb, who assures me that their opinion on Sarah's heart has not changed and that they do not believe she needs a new heart. My faith is here in Dr. Goldfarb, and with such differing points of view, we decide that this is where we will stay whatever may be.

And then it happens: Sarah gets "the call" for lungs! It's late in the night on June 11, and Dr. Goldfarb calls with the news, and we begin another night of waiting and hoping.

# 13. Transplant Day

Butterflies fill my stomach as I pace Sarah's room. It's early in the morning on June 12, 2013. Sharon arrived just a short time ago, and we see Dr. Kreindler approaching the room; everything hinges on this news, and we rush into the hallway to meet him.

Dr. Kreindler looks serious but happy, and I can tell we are about to get the news we have dreamed and hoped for, for so long.

"All the tests look good. Sarah will go into the operating room in the next couple of hours," Dr. Kreindler says cautiously.

The joy is overwhelming, and we shriek with excitement.

"I want to caution you here; there's a long road ahead of you. Sarah is very sick, and her recovery will be long and hard," he explains solemnly.

Sarah's LAS is a 94 out of 100 at this point, so his words of caution are warranted, but this does little to quell my excitement. Without these organs, there is no chance, no hope. A long, hard road is the best odds I have, and I will take them. We are told that the donor is an adult and that the lungs are in "fair" condition, but I know nothing else. I take a moment to say a prayer for this family. It's impossible not to feel their pain simultaneously with my own joy and hope. They have lost everything, and in that loss, they have decided to give someone else the world.

Over the next two to three hours, we call family, and Team Sarah notifies the media, but mostly I sit next to Sarah, hugging her and telling her the news. I hope she can hear me and that she feels the hope and relief that I feel. We did it! Sarah, of course, is still sedated, intubated, and motionless, but I tell her everything as if she is awake. I celebrate with her in my own way.

Word spreads throughout the pulmonary department, and all our favorite people come to wish her well. Time flies by quickly for me, and before I know it, there's a huge team in her room preparing her for transport. They move at lightning speed, with purpose—the clock is ticking now, I can tell. I know that once the donor lungs are removed, there is a time window in which they want to get her new lungs into her.

Her hospital bed and equipment are packed in minutes, and we begin swiftly rolling down the hallway to the operating room. I have butterflies in my stomach as I hold Sarah's hand, leaning down periodically to whisper in her ear. As we approach the operating room, Fran and I are told we can't go any farther than this point; the next stop is the OR. It's emotional, and tears well up in my eyes as I kiss her, but I feel a certainty that a world of blessings lies ahead, and my heart is filled with peace. It's odd because I always expected to be scared—terrified—at this moment, but I also never expected Sarah to be this close to death. I am not scared at all. I am elated! To me, the thing to be frightened of at this point would be not even getting the chance; at least now she has a shot at life and a future.

There are three phenomenal cardiothoracic surgeons at CHOP. Today, Thomas L. Spray, MD, chief of the Division of Cardiothoracic Surgery, is on call and will do Sarah's surgery. He is legendary at CHOP, and I know Sarah is in excellent hands despite having never met him personally. We are quickly led into his office to ask any questions of him while they prep Sarah. He is a tall, older man with kind eyes and an extremely calm disposition. His calmness is contagious, and he puts me at ease immediately.

He explains that he will determine the best way to trim the lungs once he has a visual of them; he is clearly not fazed by the prospect of resizing the donor organs. We learn that lungs from CF patients are often hard to remove due to the extensive scarring, which can cause them to adhere to the chest wall. He expects the surgery to take about six hours and asks us if we have any questions. All I can think is, *Save our kid.*

Afterward, Fran and I want so much to run to the waiting room and surround ourselves with family and rejoice, but we can't. We return to her empty hospital room, the one where we waged war with CF and the federal government, all to get to this miraculous point, and begin the daunting task of packing up her belongings once again. After the surgery, Sarah will not return to the PICU but will be in the cardiac intensive care unit (CICU). I'm relieved to be leaving the PICU. It holds a lot of sad, painful memories for me. Sarah's post-transplant room will remain bare to protect her fragile immune system post-transplant—no pictures, toys, or games—but that's OK. Anything is OK if she lives.

I can't help but look back on the long road that brought us to this place.

I was seventeen years old and Fran was nineteen when we met at a party among mutual friends. We dated on and off from that point on; he attended both my junior and senior proms. After graduation, I went to college locally, as he was already doing, and the relationship continued. From the outset, we were always very different people; Fran's calm, quiet, a bit of an introvert, while I'm definitely an extrovert and not what you would call calm or quiet at all. We balance each other most of the time. We married when I was twenty-four, and Fran just a few days shy of his twenty-seventh birthday. The relationship had been easy; I think we'd both lived pretty charmed lives up until that point.

Sarah was born three years later, just one month after my life imploded with the death of my mom. We had planned for me to stay home with Sarah, while he continued to work and get his master's degree.

Sarah's birth was relatively uncomplicated. Although she was born at thirty-six weeks' gestation, she was a big baby for her gestational age, weighing seven pounds, seven ounces. There were no red flags at her birth. She breathed normally and passed all the newborn screens.

But at home with my newborn baby, something felt wrong. She ate and ate all day and night but grew so slowly. She screamed and writhed in pain for hours. Our pediatrician dismissed me as a "first-time mom" who was overreacting. In fact, I was told that maybe she just had a cranky disposition, which I needed to accept. The pediatrician said Sarah was "so normal, she was boring." She was in the fifth percentile, and I was told she was probably just genetically small. At every turn, my concerns were dismissed. I was clearly over my head, and I felt very alone. Fran worked a full-time job and spent nights and weekends studying. The weight of Sarah's care fell predominantly to me. Despite the pediatrician saying it was unnecessary, I made an appointment with a gastro-intestinal (GI) specialist at CHOP.

The GI specialist agreed with me that something was wrong. Sarah's belly was terribly distended. She had the look of a starved child, and the doctor believed Sarah had some type of allergy, probably celiac disease. Immediately, she began Sarah on a hypoallergenic formula, Nutramigen, which is predigested. Fran and I called it "liquid gold," because it cost so much, but right away

Sarah turned the corner. She began to grow. She was still tiny, but not to a concerning degree, and the screaming and crying ceased. The relief we felt was palpable.

Finally, we began to enjoy our precious baby rather than just survive. I never knew I could love someone so much and so fiercely; motherhood was truly life-altering for me. Sarah loved to be held all the time, so that's what I did, sitting with her for hours. I would even wear her in a baby carrier as I got chores done around the house.

One day, after Sarah fell asleep in my arms, I gently transferred her to the baby swing to finally get a moment to myself. Sitting directly across from my precious girl, I shrieked with horror as I saw her turn blue; Sarah was not breathing. I grabbed her out of the swing and pounded her on the back as she gulped in air and began screaming. I can remember shaking from head to toe as I called the pediatrician, who told me to come directly over. Sarah was only four months old.

Initially, our pediatrician reacted swiftly, placing Sarah on an apnea monitor and sending me home. He assured me that everything was fine. No tests were performed, though. There was no trip to the ER. This is one of those critical moments that, when I look back, I wish I had demanded more. A week later, the same doctor who had taken me seriously by putting Sarah on a sleep apnea monitor told me he would keep Sarah on the apnea monitor but that I probably had not seen what I thought I saw that day in the swing. At that critical moment, when the pediatrician again doubted me, I realized I had stayed with the practice for too long.

So, when Sarah was four months old, I found her a new pediatrician who sang an entirely different tune. He believed something was wrong, but he was not sure what was wrong and deferred to the advice of the GI specialist. By this time, Sarah had also started with a small but consistent cough. The GI specialist believed

Sarah had severe reflux, which would explain the moment of breathlessness, and she prescribed medication for this. She explained that this reflux was the reason for Sarah's cough, too. While the cough never improved, Sarah did not have another episode of apnea and at seven months old was able to be taken off the monitor.

Trouble did not return until Sarah's first birthday, when a few things happened in tandem. We began to wean Sarah from Nutramigen to whole milk, and the pain, crying, and growth problems resumed. At the same time, Sarah caught her first real virus and had a horrendous time recovering. We would start an antibiotic and the symptoms would abate, but within a week of the conclusion of the course of antibiotics, Sarah would have what seemed to be the same raging infection again. The GI specialist again began pushing the theory that Sarah had celiac disease. Sarah had once been tested for celiac but gotten a negative result. The doctor assured us that this happens if the child has not been exposed for long enough. So again we tested. And again the results were negative. But again the doctor felt this was the accurate diagnosis; she thought maybe she had a dairy allergy, too.

During this short period of time, Sarah had a major kidney infection, which required hospitalization. She also got tubes in her ears due to repeated ear infections. She was physically uncomfortable all the time because none of the diets the GI specialist put her on were making a difference. Sarah was constantly sick even though she had virtually no exposure to germs on a regular basis. Something was wrong, and I wanted to scream at the top of my lungs. I felt terribly scared and alone.

I began researching and researching on my own. I was overwhelmed and stressed. Clearly something was seriously wrong with my child, but none of the doctors seemed capable of making an accurate diagnosis. The weight of solving this mystery was on me, and I knew it. Sarah had now had a bout with respiratory syncytial virus (RSV) that required regular nebulizer treatments; she was getting sicker and sicker.

Then, finally, my incessant research paid off. I had taken to obsessively watching the Discovery Health Channel, and one night there was a program on cystic fibrosis. Included in the show was a list of the symptoms of cystic fibrosis. I got chills. They were describing Sarah, and this was terrifying.

I slept on this discovery for several days; I did not want it to be true. I asked Lora, hoping she would tell me I was overreacting and that there was no way Sarah could have cystic fibrosis, but I got the opposite response from her, and I was crushed. Lora advised me to go to the doctor and insist that Sarah be tested for cystic fibrosis.

When I brought this up with the GI specialist at Sarah's next visit, she was dismissive, insisting that because Sarah had passed the newborn screen for cystic fibrosis she could not possibly have it. (We later learned that the newborn screen for cystic fibrosis is not accurate enough to rely on.) She added that Sarah would be off the growth charts entirely if this were the case, that Sarah was not sick enough for this devastating diagnosis. For the first time, I got pushy with a doctor and convinced her to order the test, but she was condescending and irritated with me and told me I was wrong.

On February 13, 2004, Sarah took the "gold standard" test for diagnosing cystic fibrosis—the sweat test, which is a test that measures the amount of salt (sodium chloride) in sweat. People with CF have two to five times more sodium chloride on their skin from sweating than people without CF. The next day, a Saturday and Valentine's Day, a resident from the GI department called us—not the GI specialist we had been seeing for more than a year—to tell us that Sarah tested positive for cystic fibrosis. The resident said he couldn't give me any information on what it meant or what I should do but that the pulmonary medicine department would reach out to me sometime next week, probably Monday.

My baby was diagnosed with a terminal disease, and her GI specialist did not even have the compassion to call me herself. She did not lead me to the pulmonary doctors and reassure and help me. I was left alone and devastated. Overwhelmed by this diagnosis and feeling like Monday might as well be a year away, I called the main number at CHOP and demanded to speak with the pulmonary doctor on call.

I didn't realize it at the time, but this was the moment the tide turned, when I traded callousness for experts fully prepared to stand by my side and wage war on CF. Julian Allen, MD, chief of the Division of Pulmonary Medicine, was the attending on call.

Sarah was admitted quickly to CHOP on 8-South, and a battery of tests were run. We learned a lot of hard truths, first among them that Sarah has what's called Double Delta F508, the most common type of CF and generally the most severe with the worst outcomes. Furthermore, we were told that the eighteen months without a diagnosis had cost Sarah part of one of her lungs. The damage in the lower lobe of one of her lungs was so severe and had resulted in so much scar tissue that it was unlikely that functioning of that lobe would ever be regained. Even worse, this damaged section would be a breeding ground for bacteria and would almost surely speed up her disease process.

The three weeks following Sarah's diagnosis were some of the hardest in my life. Being in that hospital room was like being in a fishbowl, with windows everywhere and people looking in while my entire life fell apart. I was given advice by professionals that was intended to help me but that left me feeling judged and criticized.

"Children do best when their parents are matter-of-fact about it [cystic fibrosis]," said one expert.

This might have been fine advice to receive a year after diagnosis, but not coming right after we had been blindsided by a terminal diagnosis and while we were still dealing with the emotions and loss that came with this. There is a day to be matter-of-fact about living with cystic fibrosis, but it is not in the first weeks after diagnosis. During those weeks, we were mourning, and we were doing this in a room in a hospital with people we didn't know looking in.

Meanwhile, Sarah was poked and prodded. She was scared and cried often, but she was too young for us to explain things to her. Fran was definitely not suited for supporting Sarah during medical procedures either. In the beginning, he would nearly pass out while Sarah got IVs. I felt during these moments that the emotional weight of supporting her fell squarely on me, although in all other aspects he was right by our side. We learned about chest physical therapy, which we initially did four times a day to try to beat back the infection that had built up in her lungs during the long period of time she had been misdiagnosed. We were taught about all the extensive medications Sarah would need, and we waited for test results that would tell us if any other organs were damaged. Waiting for the answer to that question was terrifying. How much worse could it get?

Dr. Allen was kind and compassionate. He was the attending on service for the first week Sarah was hospitalized. He worked nonstop and could be found in the hallways sometimes at eleven o'clock at night. He answered all my questions, and despite my being a complete wreck, I never once felt judged by him. Sarah was terrified, and he patiently tried to perform her exams as she screamed and cried.

Eighteen-month-old Sarah began to react to people showing up at our door by crying out fearfully, "All done, all done!" before they could reach her bed. Too many people came in to poke and prod her. She blew intravenous lines (IVs) regularly, meaning the vein would rupture or get punctured and could no longer be used, and therefore had more than a handful of IVs placed as she awaited surgery for a PICC line placement. A PICC line is like an IV except it gives vein access to larger veins closer to the heart. Sarah always had hers placed in her upper arm.

Sarah needed to stay in the hospital for several weeks, and at the beginning of the second week, we got a new attending pulmonologist on 8-South. His name was Howard Panitch, who I described earlier, and I was struck by how much he listened to me. When I told him what I saw in Sarah's response to treatment, he treated it as fact and reacted accordingly. My fears started to subside at least slightly.

Dr. Panitch won Sarah over, too. He saw her love of Elmo and came in on day two with an Elmo tie and put an Elmo sticker on his nose. He made the fellows talk like Cookie Monster and crawled over to Sarah where she was sitting on the floor in my lap. For the first time, Sarah did not scream, and he was able to listen to her lungs. By the end of the week, she was sitting on his lap.

I was an emotional wreck and had millions of questions, but Dr. Panitch accepted this. He never rushed us; he allowed me to ask all my questions day after day. And each day, Sarah improved little by little.

I was very type A about Sarah's care (I still am). I had and still have very high expectations of everyone who deals with her and very high expectations of myself. I decided that if I worked hard enough and gave Sarah perfect care, we would get a better outcome than the ones the doctors were describing. In this regard, Dr. Panitch and I were a perfect match; he was (and is) type A, too, with very high expectations of everyone dealing with Sarah as well.

After three weeks, we were allowed to go home. Sarah was assigned to an attending physician who had not treated Sarah in the hospital, but I asked to switch to Dr. Panitch, and my request was honored.

In the months before Sarah's diagnosis, when I had not found a good doctor to help Sarah, I had developed a twitch in my eye—an uncontrollable spasm—in anticipation of any doctor appointment. I believe this was because I felt such tremendous responsibility for getting her the right medical care though I had none of the training or knowledge of a doctor. One week after we went home, we returned for our first outpatient visit, and for the first time in months, my eye did not twitch. I believe this is because I had turned over Sarah's care to Dr. Panitch—not only physically but emotionally as well.

My dad was critical in this last step for me, which helped my sanity immensely. He said, "Do your research and work hard to find the right doctor, hospital, and team. Once you have found them, trust them."

I handed over Sarah's care to Dr. Panitch and trusted him, and he never let us down. He treated Sarah aggressively, and I followed the path he set in front of me diligently, but it was clear from the start that the damage to Sarah's lung would be more than a thorn in our side.

Meanwhile, Fran needed to work and continue school, and there was a distance between us and a resentment in me for what he had, a life away from the hospitals and tests. It really wasn't a fair resentment; after all, I wanted to be the stay-at-home parent, and we made sacrifices so that I could do that, but this wasn't what I had envisioned.

There were a lot of medical decisions to be made, and as the parent who attended all the appointments, I was in the best position to make those decisions. I felt a huge sense of guilt for the first year and a half of Sarah not being diagnosed. I was the one who had been there; I should have known or pushed harder. Fran never felt any of this was true, he never put that on me, but I did, and now I felt this enormous burden of having to make all these life-and-death decisions. I felt alone.

We had new questions about how we would continue to grow our family faced with the knowledge that any child we conceived would have a one-in-four chance of having CF. We struggled to agree on how we would move forward.

The next several years after Sarah's diagnosis were some of the hardest in my life. I won't detail every decision Fran and I made together, but I'll say the biggest thing we learned to do, and the reason I think our marriage survived, was accept who each other was.

Fran really wasn't that comfortable with blood and medical procedures, and instead of holding on to my frustration, I made a conscience decision to let it go. I was by default the one who needed to make most of the medical decisions, because I was the one who was there. I needed to not put my anxiety about that on him, because he never faulted me or acted like I made the wrong choices. When we couldn't find common ground, the person who felt more passionately won the day, and over time this worked.

We fell into a routine. I definitely did not take care of Sarah at home on my own. Fran and I both worked hard with medication and chest physical therapy to keep her safe and healthy, but doctors' visits and the hospital became my domain with Fran coming as much as he could. We accepted each other, and over the years, Fran's aversion to all things blood and medical faded dramatically. And my fears about being in charge were replaced with confidence and even an inability by the end not to be the one in charge.

We worked it out. Grew our family. Life was hard, but by the time Sarah was five, we had three kids and a good routine for handling the hospital and crisis.

Our life got into a rhythm. There was "normal" mode where we had the typical chaos of family life coupled with two hours of chest physical therapy and multiple medications daily. Then we had "hospital" mode. Sarah was hospitalized every couple of months. We figured it out, life stabilized, and we had our own sense of normal.

By the age of six, Sarah was diagnosed with a bacterium called *Mycobacterium avium-intracellulare* infection (MAI). We knew this was bad news. The progression of lung disease in patients with cystic fibrosis is directly related to the bacteria the patients acquire and how deadly these bacteria are. MAI is a bad one—not seen often in children as young as Sarah—and combined with her severe lung damage, it put her on a terrible trajectory.

We aggressively tried to eradicate this bacterium, but we knew our chances were not good. Sarah's lung damage had created scar tissue that would be a breeding ground and hiding place for the bacterium. Sarah's appetite decreased dramatically, and she required the insertion of a G-tube and all-night feeds to help her gain weight and continue to grow. Even with the excessive calories from these feeds, Sarah's weight and height barely budged. Her body was using all this food energy to battle the infections inside her.

By the age of seven, Sarah required a port catheter, which is a small device placed under the skin that gave direct access to larger veins for people who require frequent IVs. At this point, Sarah was being hospitalized every two to three months. We tried hard to keep life as "normal" as possible, but it was an uphill battle.

We failed to eliminate the MAI despite our valiant effort, and Sarah's lung function inched southward. Eventually, I took Sarah to Colorado for a second opinion, and the doctors there told me what I already believed—that CHOP was doing everything that could be done. We were told Sarah would likely be a candidate for lung transplant in her early teens.

When Sarah was nine years old and in third grade, everything took a dramatic turn for the worse. The medication, which had been holding the bacteria at bay, stopped working. Her bacteria had become resistant and was now in control. Sarah's lung function dropped to 30 percent, and she went on full-time oxygen and was listed for transplant.

Now, after a painfully long wait for donor lungs, we wait for our baby to return to us from surgery. Sarah has received the gift of life that we pray will be a new beginning.

## Fran

We have an offer! Now, this is our fourth offer, so I am a bit more cautious in my optimism. Dr. Kreindler says the lungs are good enough, and that is all I need to hear.

Dr. Spray is a world-renowned surgeon, and CHOP is a world-renowned hospital, so if the team says it is a go, we are on board. We have been working with CHOP since Sarah was one and a half years old, and they have never let us down in the end.

Even though the surgery is obviously a serious one, I am excited. It's the news we've been waiting for. I am not completely on edge. I am feeling relieved. We have waited what seems a lifetime for this one moment, and it is here.

# 14. Code Blue

The surgical waiting room for lung transplant and cardiac patients is separate from the general surgery waiting room. It's smaller and more intimate, situated close to the cardiac operating rooms and just outside the cardiac ICU where Sarah will go after surgery. A large TV hangs from the wall; a coffee machine, snacks, and free drinks fill the fridge. It feels more like a small family room or family lounge than a surgical waiting area. Although intimate, there's ample seating for more than one family, but we are the only ones here today, filling the room almost completely. Trying to distract myself, I flick through the channels landing on CNN, and an ethics "expert" is criticizing the ruling that allowed Sarah access to these organs. Ugh, I want to scream! I am so infuriated watching this nobody claim my daughter deserves to die, because that's the sum of it. Fuming, I turn the TV off and return to my scattered thoughts and bouncing legs.

As the hours tick by, my nerves finally start to get the best of me. The initial euphoria fades, and I start to think of all the what-ifs. Six hours is a long, long time when your baby's life is on the line. Periodically, someone comes out to update us; we are told that the CF lungs are finally out and that it was a difficult removal, as the doctor had anticipated. This is one hurdle down, and I breathe my first sigh of relief.

Knowing that I have a long day still ahead of me, I take a break and step outside into the warm sunshine. It is almost shocking to feel the heat on my face; it has been at least a week since I came outside to do my last interview. The street outside the hospital is lined with media, and I walk over unannounced to take interviews.

Maureen, Tracy, Sharon, and I have already determined that after transplant, Sharon will be the only one available for interviews. If there is an overwhelming need, Tracy and Maureen can step in, but no one doubts that this is the last time I will be outside and away from Sarah for a long time.

Claire is still holding things together at Sharon's house with all our kids. It's a relief to be able to tell them that their sister is getting a transplant. My second and third graders were told on the school bus recently that their sister is dying. We had intentionally screened them from all media coverage, but a few of their classmates' parents told their kids, and these kids relayed the news to mine. Who does this? Sean responded by telling the kids they were wrong and mean and to "shut up." Ella believed what they said, and tears and devastation followed. So, telling them the news that Sarah was getting lungs was pure joy.

Finally, surgical staff come out with the best news of all. Sarah is out of surgery; the surgery has been deemed a success, and Dr. Spray will meet with us shortly. The tears just spill out as I walk to a special room and wait for a detailed update from the surgeon. Sharon and Team Sarah get to work notifying the media; the world is celebrating with us today.

Shaking my leg incessantly, I sit impatiently waiting for Dr. Spray to arrive. Fran is quiet as usual. Our approaches to everything are complete opposites. Dr. Spray arrives looking exhausted. I am struck by what a sacrifice his career must be. His words are calm and deliberate.

"Everything went well. There were no complications, although her CF lungs were challenging to remove as I expected," he explains. "My team is settling Sarah into her room in the CICU, where she will be watched around the clock for any complications. The first hours are the most critical. Someone will come get you soon, so just sit tight."

"Thank you so much," I say as I reach out and hug him.

True to character, as soon as Dr. Spray leaves, I sneak down the hallway to get a brief glance at my girl. Fran is powerless to stop me, although he tries. He is much more of a rule follower than I am.

There are at least thirty people in and around her room. Everyone is calm and deliberate, and no one notices me. In the middle of the room lies my sweet, precious girl. She is connected to a pile of tubes, wires, and monitors; she looks puffy and pale, but it is definitely her. She is alive! It's a relief to catch a glimpse of her, and I quickly and quietly head back to the waiting room before anyone notices me.

I expect to be brought back to her room quickly, but no one comes. Sharon returns from a marathon of media interviews and is surprised to see us still waiting. Everyone else in the family has been sent home because they won't be able to see Sarah today. I suppose this waiting game is just how it goes, but with each minute that passes, my nerves begin to get the best of me.

Finally, Dr. Goldfarb pops his head in. He looks tired, stressed, and rushed—very uncharacteristic of him. I'm sure it's been a hard day.

"Sarah's struggling a little. I'd like to do a bronchoscopy on her lungs right now to see if there is an obvious cause. Can you sign this consent?" He is clearly rushed, and we sign quickly without any questions.

I know the first hours are critical and often bumpy, but now I am panicking. I have seldom seen Dr. Goldfarb stressed. He is very cool under pressure, confident. I desperately want to go down to Sarah's room, but Fran is holding me back.

"We need to stay out of the way and let them do their job," he says sternly.

"Me standing in the hallway is not going to stop anyone from doing their job." I'm angry now, but I sit back and wait. *God, what is happening? What's wrong? Please, God, guide them and let my baby live.*

I think it's close to midnight now. They took Sarah around noon. It has been a tremendously long day, and my nerves are shot. I'm telling myself not to worry. *The first hours post-transplant are hard. They have always told us that. She is in great hands. This should be a day of joy, Janet, relax.*

I've grown so accustomed to expecting the worst news because, frankly, that's all I've gotten for the longest time. I need to stop, relax, and accept the fact that we did it. We are here in this moment I have prayed and hoped for, for so long. But dread fills my body. I can't help feeling like something is very wrong.

I want to hold her hand and reassure her that she is going to be OK. What am I doing sitting here endlessly waiting? I can't stand sitting in this waiting room any longer. And then it happens.

The loudspeakers blare throughout the hospital, sirens sounding. "Code blue, code blue, sixth floor, main hospital. Code blue, code blue." The sound is deafening. Doctors, woken from sleep, charge past our waiting room in flip-flops and scrubs. The sirens sound, "Emergency ECMO team, sixth floor, main hospital."

I scream, "It's Sarah! That's her room!" And I charge down the hallway, not waiting for a response from Sharon or Fran, who chase after me. Fran is shouting, "It's not her! It's OK!"

But as we turn the corner, my world crumbles. People are flooding in and out of Sarah's room. Orders are being called out in a deliberate but race-against-time tone. I stand frozen outside her doorway. I can't see her. I see a resuscitation bag through the mass and blur of people and orders. Large equipment goes whizzing by me.

I fall to the floor outside her room, silently screaming in my head. I'm powerless as they struggle to keep Sarah alive. I know she is dying!

I'm frozen in horror. Fran and Sharon are next to me. A nurse comes up next to me and kindly and gently tries to coax me to walk away. She doesn't want me to see this; she doesn't want this to be the last vision I ever have of my baby.

"Please let me take you to the family waiting area. You shouldn't be here; you don't want to watch this."

I don't look in her direction. My eyes are frozen on the organized chaos struggling to keep my baby from dying. I can see Dr. Goldfarb and Dr. Kreindler in the room. The anesthesiologist who'd wheeled her to the operating room is bagging her. There's blood. Where is the blood coming from?

"If you want me to leave, you will need to call security," I say.

I can't see what's happening. I can't see Sarah through the flood of people and equipment. Time slows! I realize they have assigned staff, maybe nurses or residents, to stand by us. Do they think I'm going to charge the room or collapse?

My child is dying! Doctors call out orders to each other in a calm and decisive manner. Everyone knows their role; they have trained for this.

Finally, the commotion slows, and a handful of people start to leave the room. No one has called her death. She must still be alive. *Oh, God, please let her live, please.*

And then a solemn Dr. Goldfarb and Dr. Kreindler walk toward us. Dr. Goldfarb starts.

"Sarah was stable when she returned from the operating room but quickly started to decline, which is why I performed the bronchoscopy. It's clear that all the surgical sutures are in place; it's not a flaw in the surgery or anything we can fix by going back into the operating room. The lungs themselves are failing—graft failure." His expression and tone of voice are grave.

Dr. Goldfarb explains that primary graft dysfunction is more common than graft failure and occurs in about 10–25 percent of lung transplants. Most patients recover from it, but Sarah has a severe case that they believe has progressed quickly to graft failure. The chance of survival in cases of graft failure is minimal. They believe that in Sarah's case, her chances of death without new lungs is 100 percent.

"We did an X-ray, and the lungs are entirely white; there's no ventilation. At this point, her heart has stopped, too," Dr. Kreindler clarifies. "We were able to place her on a heart-lung bypass machine called VA ECMO, which has taken over the work of her heart and lungs temporarily."

He explains that VA ECMO is not a permanent solution and that Sarah can live this way for only about seven to twenty-one days. "The team is relisting her for transplant right now. Our best chance would be another match," explains Dr. Goldfarb.

"There's no chance that these lungs will recover? I don't understand," I stammer.

"I'm afraid that's highly unlikely. Graft failure like this is usually deadly. It means the lungs were likely damaged before they were removed from the donor in a manner not detected by our initial screening. I'm so sorry," he explains.

"If she lives, will she be brain damaged? Did she lose a lot of oxygen?" I ask, panicked.

"We don't know. It's possible," Dr. Kreindler responds gently. The answer hangs in the air like a noose around my neck.

"We won't be leaving the floor for a while. We are at the main desk if you need us. The team is finishing up, and you will be allowed to be with her soon," Dr. Goldfarb says as he turns to go.

"What do you want me to do, Jan and Fran?" Sharon asks.

In that moment, it's very clear to me that this is it. I ask her to call our priest, Matt Holcombe. "Ask him to come right away. She's dying. Don't call anyone else or tell anyone else. If we lose her now, we do so privately and alone. There will be a time later to tell people. Right now, I need to be solely focused on Sarah."

Fran agrees.

Moments later, we are ushered into her brightly lit hospital room. Sarah is hooked up to a large machine, which is circulating all her blood outside her body. It's an almost medieval-looking contraption. The scariest thing I have ever seen. Sarah is perfectly still and silent. There's no rise and fall of her chest, her heart doesn't beat. I hug and kiss her, and I know we might lose her.

## Fran

I will never forget the scene in Sarah's room after the code blue is called. It is an organized chaos with people rushing in and out of the room. The steady player in the room is a woman at the top of the bed behind Sarah's head who is using a vent bag to push air into Sarah's new lungs. Then the scene starts to slow in pace, and I can hear some people discussing that they "have her" and that she is stabilizing. She is alive.

Then we get the news from Dr. Goldfarb that even though she has been stabilized, she has been put on VA ECMO. Her new lungs have failed. I am totally lost at this point, not understanding what has happened. Dr. Goldfarb explains that she is on VA ECMO, which is doing the job of her lungs and heart, that she is going back on the lung transplant list, but mostly all I hear is "Blah, blah, blah."

We have never been in a worse position than now. I take a deep breath and start to sort out this new reality. I know I need to stay focused and move forward. Someone brings up the topic of all the people outside the hospital, who know Sarah received a transplant and believe it was a success. Our Sarah has become big news, not only in the United States but around the world. But I cannot deal with that right now. And I cannot deal with our extended family either. My recommendation is that we just focus on Sarah and nothing else. The reality is that the whole picture may change again by morning, most likely for the worse.

By the way, today was our wedding anniversary. Happy anniversary to me and Janet.

# 15. ECMO

When I walk into Sarah's hospital room, the lights are blazing; everything feels lit up, even though it is probably after midnight. Sarah is lying completely still on a bed positioned in the middle of the room, which is surrounded by machines, tubes, and wires. The doctors have placed Sarah on ECMO. This is not the type of ECMO they had discussed putting Sarah on in the past, awake and exercising, that would have bypassed just her lungs. This type of ECMO is referred to as VA ECMO, and it bypasses Sarah's lungs and her heart, and all the blood flow is diverted through the ECMO circuit. Sarah's heart and lungs are not working at all; both are completely still, completely silent. She is fully—and heavily—sedated for this.

The ECMO circuit looks like some type of medieval contraption, not high-tech enough to be the only thing standing between Sarah and death. This machine terrifies me. The first thing I notice are the thick, heavy tubes protruding from Sarah's neck where they connect to a vital artery. Only sutures seem to be holding these tubes in place. Through the tubes courses a continuous flow of blood in and out of Sarah. The blood winds and twists in and out of different chambers of the machine's circuit in a sort of circular fashion, trying to replicate the work of Sarah's heart and lungs. The tubes coming out of her neck are attached to such vital arteries that I am panicked each time we need to shift or reposition her body. What if they come loose or break? Would the blood flow be stoppable? Could simply bumping her the wrong way cause her to bleed to death? It's the stuff nightmares are made of!

Sitting in the center of this mass of blood tubes and wires is my baby. Everything about Sarah looks puffy and swollen. She is motionless and pale, no rise and fall of her chest, no heart beating; it is a horrifying sight, and I fear that my Sarah is not there anymore. A long white bandage goes across her entire chest covering the massive incision where they cut her entirely open to save her life. Four tubes are coming out of her chest wall as well, with a bloody fluid draining into canisters beside her bed. Even though her lungs have stopped working, there is a tube that goes up her nose and down her throat into her lungs. Holding it in place is thick tape plastered across her face. A giant IV pole with dozens of medications blinks and periodically beeps as it sends different kinds of medications simultaneously through her veins. This is extreme life support, medical intervention the likes of which you could not find just anywhere.

Sarah looks so different, like she has been through a war. It is obvious that people have worked on her. Even though she isn't awake and crying, we can see that her body has been put through the wringer, so to speak. And now these lungs don't work. I look at her and think, *How does this go somewhere good?*

I spent all day expecting to walk into this room and see my girl breathing with new lungs—with machines at first, of course—within reach of independent life and breathing. And now I am in such a different place. I am back to that place where I'm going to lose her, only now I am certain of it.

We are not alone with her. Staying for the long haul tonight is a kind fellow, with a great Australian accent, whom we will grow to trust; a phenomenal nurse, who holds herself and the team to extremely high standards; and the person running the ECMO circuit, whose job, it seems, is to stare at this machine nonstop and tweak it here and there as it circulates Sarah's blood. It is like the fishbowl experience of our first hospital stay after her diagnosis with one major difference—I no longer care who is watching me as I crumble. All self-consciousness is lost. Fran and Sharon are there for this horror as well.

Maneuvering around the mess of tubes and wires, I sit as close to Sarah as I can get. I hold her perfectly still hand in mine and put my head down next to her and just pray. My prayers are not that articulate or coherent anymore. I'm begging. *Oh my God, please let her be OK. Don't leave us, please. I can't do this alone. Please stay with us, please.*

Looking at her, I wonder, *Could we ever get to the other side of this? Is there any way? Even if we re-transplanted her, what is left of Sarah? Everything? Nothing?* It's so hard for me to imagine things ever being OK again.

### Fran

ECMO is much worse than I ever could have imagined it. The machine looks like it was built during World War II from spare parts bought from a local hardware store. I wish I were exaggerating, but I am not. The room is very bright, and the machine is manned 24–7 to ensure it runs correctly.

There is a big cannula protruding from Sarah's neck. It links into her carotid artery. Then, not some, but all of her blood flows out of her body, through a bunch of tubes, is oxygenated, and then put back into her body. That simple. Not! They have to clamp and unclamp one of the tubes periodically to prevent blood clots from forming. A blood clot is one of the many ways death can occur.

As always, Janet and I start to ask questions, which is not always the most comforting path forward, but we always prefer to live in reality, no matter how unreal and terrible reality may feel at the moment. It seems the other significant issue they watch carefully for is if the circuit fails. Well, the backup circuit kicks in, right? *No!* Which part is the circuit, exactly? Oh, the big tube sticking out of her neck, the one with all the blood flowing through it. Well, it makes sense you don't want it to fail.

Tonight, Sarah essentially died before us and then came back to life, but barely. It's surreal. I'm struggling to get a grip on where we are now and what's next.

Outside of the immediate hospital staff, only Janet, Sharon, Lora, myself, and our priest know what is going on. Janet decided it was time to call the priest, which pretty much explains just how bad things really are at this point.

It quickly becomes clear that we are in a marathon, not a sprint. Either new lungs will come very soon or we will lose Sarah. Sarah needs a parent around the clock still, so again we decide to divide and conquer.

Our priest, Reverend Matt Holcombe, arrives. He seems so calm and so sure. He is not sure that she is going to live, but sure that if she doesn't live, she will be OK, somewhere better. I feel totally devastated and destroyed but simultaneously surrounded by God's love. I'm not expecting a miracle; I just need to feel God's presence in this moment, because I believe with my whole heart that this is good-bye, and I want to be certain that she goes directly from my arms into God's.

At this point, Sharon and Fran go to a family sleep room to

finally get some rest. Lora has been sent home to help Claire keep the kids in good cheer, and Matt and I stay by Sarah's side. He prays for her as he and I stand by her bed. Matt helps me feel closer to God during this impossible time. Somehow, he brings some peace into this horror for me. So even though I am nowhere close to being OK, I have a peace right now that God's here and that as Sarah transitions to heaven, she will go from my arms to his. Matt's prayers and presence have brought me that peace.

After a while, we sit down on the bench in Sarah's room. Matt tells me about how he chose to become a priest after a career in the layman's world. We sit just behind the machine circulating all the blood; the lights still blare, and the doctor, nurse, and ECMO specialist remain. In the past, I have mostly wanted to be alone, to shield my pain from anyone who is not immediate and intimate family. This is the worst night of my life, and I am here with all these people, and I find that it is comforting not to be alone. The doctor responds calmly to my many questions, as does everyone here, and I feel that despite the horrifying situation, Sarah is in the best hands physically and spiritually. Sarah is in the best hands, no matter what comes next. I think of all the moments leading up to this moment, and this is the one, more than any other, where I am the most certain that it is the end. I have no hope left for her life.

## Reverend Matt Holcombe

The ringing phone wakes me up.

For several weeks, I have been sleeping with my phone next to my bed, waiting for this phone call. The phone screen tells me that the caller is Sharon Ruddock. Oh no! I do my best to sound awake as I answer the phone. Sharon simply says, "We need you to come now. There were complications with the transplant."

I assure her I am on my way and hang up the phone. My wife asks if everything is OK with Sarah. I shake my head and assure her that I will call her when I know more. I get dressed, and as I put on my black clergy shirt and collar, I realize I'm putting on the armor of God in a way that I have not before. As I tie my shoes, I find myself praying for peace—for Sarah, Janet, Fran, Sharon, Lora, the doctors, the nurses, and the family that gave the gift of hope through a set of lungs.

As I walk into the darkness of the night and get into my car, I am greeted by stillness and silence. I am scared for what may be coming. I begin driving. I have been to the hospital dozens of times over the past several months. The route is familiar, but the prayers and thoughts in my head are much different for this drive from those of others. Twenty minutes later, I arrive at the hospital. It is past midnight, but news vans and cameramen are parked in front of the hospital, as they have been since the news of Sarah's fight made national headlines.

I walk through the lobby and straight past security. I imagine the security guards waved me past because they know a priest doesn't show up at the hospital past midnight unless the news is bad.

Stepping off the elevator on the sixth floor was unfamiliar for me. I have grown accustomed to the eighth floor and Sarah's normal room, where she has a wall of windows looking out over a construction site. In the months I have been visiting, the building across the street has gone from a hole in the ground to a massive ten-floor structure.

I turn the corner on the unfamiliar sixth floor and see Janet, Fran, and Sharon all standing in the hallway. From down the hall, I can see the terror and defeat on their faces. I embrace each of them and receive an update on Sarah's condition and prognosis. It is not good. Soon after arriving, Janet convinces Fran and Sharon to go get some sleep. After Fran and Sharon leave, Janet asks if I want to see Sarah.

Nothing in my training or hundreds of hospital visits as a priest could prepare me for what I am about to see. Lying amid what seem like miles of wires and tubes is the motionless, breathless, lifeless body of a little girl. She has some resemblance to Sarah with the same nose and eyebrows and same color hair, but that is about all. Janet explains the VA ECMO machine and how it is doing all the work for Sarah so her body can rest. As I watch the ECMO machine draw blood in and out of her body, it is as if I am watching a machine be God. I marvel at the human hands who have perfected this ECMO technology and all those surrounding Sarah as they use the gifts they have been given by God to help and serve others.

Janet and I stay in Sarah's room for hours. We pray with Sarah and over Sarah. We pray for the donor who has given Sarah her first pair of lungs. We pray for the doctors and nurses. We pray for the surgeons and those who transported the lungs. We pray for Sarah's brothers and sister. We pray for hope.

Eventually, we find ourselves sitting next to Sarah as a constant parade of nurses and doctors comes in and out of the room checking on machines, pressing buttons, and checking on their patient. Janet and I talk about life, death, and our families. Nothing is off-limits. I share my story about becoming a priest and how Paul's letter to the Corinthians provided me with guidance when I needed it the most. I reveal that it was realizing "God's power is made perfect in my weakness" (2 Corinthians 12:9) and that through my weakness, my reliance in God is transformed into something far greater and better than I could ever imagine. Even if this passage does not provide Janet with comfort, it selfishly is a good reminder for me.

As the hours melt away, Sarah continues to lie in the same bed she coded in hours prior. However, as time goes on, I find Janet with a renewed sense of peace—not because everything is going to turn out the way Janet and Fran have imagined but because Sarah is in good hands and she is at peace.

As the sun slowly rises and word comes from the doctors and nurses that Sarah has been added back onto the transplant list, there is a sense of new hope and a chance for another new beginning. Before I leave Sarah's side, we pray and give thanks to God for a new day. Not that any of us know what the day will bring, but that God has just given us front-row tickets to a miracle.

The next morning, after Matt leaves, Sarah's transplant physician, Dr. Goldfarb, comes in and confirms that there is no hope for these lungs. He reiterates that she can only live on ECMO for a short period of time.

"If you get an offer for lungs, don't tell me. Please don't tell me until you are coming to wheel her down the hallway. OK? I will take any organ that you think is viable, but I cannot emotionally survive the ups and downs of losing an offer, so don't tell me until you are certain."

"OK," he says.

I know I could not live through the devastation of getting another offer and then losing it or losing her before it came to fruition. I don't believe it will happen, so I don't want anyone to give me hope at this point. Getting to this point of no hope broke me completely. The idea that I could hope again—that I could believe in a future that includes Sarah—only to lose her again is something I know I would not survive emotionally.

# 16. Waiting

The next few days tick by slowly. There is nothing to differentiate them. Sarah is sedated, intubated, unmoving, and—I fear—already gone. The machines whir, the lights glare, and there are always people in and out of the room keeping a close watch on her. An ECMO specialist is always sitting there staring at and tweaking the machine; a nurse is either in the room or sitting at the desk outside the room where she can watch Sarah through a window. As they tweak the ECMO circuit here and there, we watch, we wait, we watch some more, and we pray. There is nothing else we can do.

It is impossible to believe that we could get the gift of life again after waiting eighteen months to finally get the first set of lungs. A second set is an impossibility; it seems unrealistic and unlikely.

We have not told anyone about the failure of Sarah's transplant. We have made a conscious decision to hold on to the privacy. We haven't even called Sarah's grandparents. We haven't called the kids. The thought of telling them is unbearable. I simply do not want anybody else to live through this hell—this uncertainty, this slow death—with us if they don't have to. To me, it is a gift I am giving to them to not include them in this horror. There will be a time for that. There's no rush for the sadness to come. So, we sit, we watch, and we wait alone.

Fran and I take shifts. Sharon is still here, too. So, there are almost always two people awake. Unlike before transplant, Sarah's sedation is deep and there is no concern that she will wake, but we stand vigil by her side anyway.

The team in the CICU is tremendous, starting with the nurses, who almost never have Sarah out of their sight and treat her with gentle love and care. There are strict rules on this floor. For example, if a monitor beeps, we can't silence it and then go get our nurse, as we have always done on every other floor. We are not allowed to touch it; we are not allowed to do a thing. In fact, I get the impression that if I violate this rule, I will be screamed at, but this is OK; an overly protective staff is exactly what we need right now, and I suppose, that's the case for everyone who finds themselves on this floor.

For the first time, I try to go to the parent room to sleep, because it is hard to sleep in a brightly lit room with a constant stream of people, all of whom seem to be required for the ECMO circuit. After tossing and turning for a little over an hour, I quickly decide that this will never work for me. As a result, I don't sleep for a couple of days, except for quick naps on a bench in Sarah's room, with virtual sunshine raining down on me.

This moment in time is indescribable—the level of pain and anguish, the sheer terror. Sarah's lovely team from 8-South, who have known Sarah her whole life and cheered her on, believe she is recovering well from a great lung transplant, and they come to the floor in groups to congratulate us and cheer us on. These are the best people. But I am not prepared to share this or live through this with anyone else, and I am not sure what to say or how to deal with it. I don't invite them into the room or give any details, and I am quick with them. I don't say, "These lungs don't work, and they never will. This is good-bye." I haven't even told my family this. I can't tell the nursing staff. I'm not sure I am even capable of saying those words out loud. These are the people who have loved and cared for Sarah; these are our friends. It feels wrong, like a betrayal, to shut them out, but I do just that. I shut the world out. All my friends who have worked so hard to save Sarah, everyone. I can't deal with anybody's emotions other than my own right now.

Fran is very quiet. He is basically speechless. Sharon is very solution-driven. "How can I help you? What can I do?" Whatever emotions Sharon feels in this situation, which I know are tremendous having lost her own child, she does not show them. We sit and wait, but we don't expect anything, at least not anything good. I am tormented.

Sarah has been relisted for lungs, but her new LAS score is lower than before even though she is even closer to dying now. Prior to Sarah's first transplant, I believe her score was a 94, which is just about as high of a priority as a person can be. Now her score is an 89, I believe. At first, I think this is odd, but Dr. Goldfarb explains that the calculation considers survivability. Sarah's odds of surviving are lower now, so her LAS is lower. He explains that someone waiting for transplant who is equally as sick but hasn't been through the trauma Sarah has been through has a higher chance of surviving and therefore a higher priority. This makes sense to me.

It must be hard allocating these organs, essentially deciding who lives and who dies through a complex algorithm that often does not do good by individuals. It is a flawed system for sure. But today's news makes sense; she has lower odds of making it out of the OR alive if she gets an offer. I know Sarah's score is still very high and that it is unlikely that anyone in our region has that high of a score anyway, but I am no longer analyzing the data. The reality is I have no hope of any kind.

Three days pass, and we know she can't live for long on this ECMO circuit. Certainly, we must be near the end. And then the unexpected happens; they come to us and say they have lungs for Sarah. They have known all night but respected my request and are only telling us now because Sarah is only a couple of hours away from going into the operating room. Doctors are on-site; they are already awaiting retrieval; final tests on the lungs have already been performed; and the medical team has accepted them as a match for Sarah.

There is hope, but a very somber, cautious hope in the air. It is not the same news that it was getting the first lungs. Unlike the first set of lungs, which we were told were in good-enough condition, we are told this set of lungs is not. The donor has been intubated and sedated for a long time, and due to the endotracheal tube (ET) down the donor's throat, the donor has pneumonia in a section of one of the lungs. The donor, however, is a blood match, a match in the things that would make her body reject or not reject, and in all likelihood, this is our last chance.

I try to imagine the donor's family, who fought like hell and lost their loved one anyway. For the second time, someone is giving us this gift, and I pray for them. They don't give you any details about the donor.

The mood is quiet as they gently lay out all the problems they will face once in the operating room. A lot could go wrong. Sarah needs to come off the ECMO circuit and be placed on bypass. The new lungs need to be resized to work for her. Then her heart, which has been still for three days, must restart. There is a lot that could go wrong. Dr. Kreindler is explaining it all to me, and I have no delusions; this is not a pessimistic description—this is reality. He does not belabor it. I don't think anybody, at this point, thinks that I don't get it. That we don't get it. The odds that this will end well are slim. These are lungs that in almost any other circumstance they would turn down. But given the window of time that we have left, this is it. It's not the best of odds, but it's better than nothing.

So, while we have a speck of hope, there is no elation or joy, just fear. We don't call the family—the family still does not know; they are still basking in the success and joy of the first transplant. Only Fran, myself, Sharon, and Lora will carry the weight of today and the implications for Sarah's future.

Just before surgery, Dr. Spray comes into the room and asks us if we have any questions.

"Is there any hope here that she lives?" I blurt out.

"*Yes!*" he says. "Yes, if Sarah was certainly going to die, I would not take her into the operating room. I don't take children to the operating room to die." They are the most reassuring words I have ever heard. Dr. Spray's confidence exudes to his patients. It's a gift.

"But they say the donor has pneumonia. I don't understand. She doesn't have an immune system. What's going to happen when we give her lungs with pneumonia?" I ask.

His answers are very simple, straightforward, and to the point.

"I have to resize the lungs anyway, so I won't use that portion of the lung. Sarah's young; her body is otherwise strong and resilient." Little by little, Dr. Spray gives me the seeds of hope that will carry me for the next few hours as I wait for Sarah to come out of surgery. It might still be possible.

After this conversation, I do feel more hopeful. I don't feel like I did last time. There is no joy and elation; there is no vision of a perfect ending. There is just this dim glow of hope that something might be possible, but I don't know what that something is.

True to their word, not a lot of time passes before Sarah is once again being wheeled toward the OR. We don't coast swiftly down the hallway this time; we inch at a gentle, deliberate pace with an enormous team and tons of equipment, most notable of which is an ECMO circuit.

I kiss her before she goes back for surgery, but unlike last time, I don't believe she can hear me. I don't necessarily feel like she is there. I don't know where she is, but it's hard to look at her, totally still with no rise or fall of the chest, with no heart beating, puffy and swollen, and to imagine she is still in there. But I pray that she is!

Dr. Spray explains that the surgery will be shorter than the last transplant. This time the lung removal will not be complex but quick and easy. So, we are told to expect it to take about four hours.

Sharon, Fran, and I go to the same family waiting room. It's just the three of us anxiously waiting. As the time passes, surgical nurses periodically come in and out to give us updates. They are very cautious updates, but each one moves us a step forward, because it lets us know they haven't lost her.

After about four hours, we get the news we have been praying for—surgery is over and Sarah is alive, with new lungs and successfully off bypass, heart beating and all. We are led to the same little room to await a detailed update from Dr. Spray.

When he arrives, Dr. Spray is clearly happy with the results. We know she is not out of the woods yet, but she has cleared a major obstacle.

In his clear and calm manner, he tells me one of the most surprising things I have ever been told.

"Before you go to see her, you should be aware that I've left her open," he says very matter-of-factly.

And I say, "Open? What part of her open?"

"All of her. Her entire chest is open. There's a thin film of bandage protecting her, but her entire chest is open."

Over the next several minutes, he explains how terribly swollen Sarah is from the back-to-back surgeries. If he closed her chest now, the pressure would collapse the new lungs. The only other alternative would be to shave the lungs down and make them thinner; however, that does not produce as good an outcome as a simple lobectomy.

"In a week, we will take her back in the OR and close her. I'm confident that the swelling will be down enough that we will not need to trim the lungs further. In the meantime, she will remain heavily sedated," he explains.

As we approach Sarah's bed, it quickly becomes obvious that the protective film over the opening leaves little to the imagination. We can see the squeezing of her heart as it beats and the rise and fall of her lungs. It is shocking, but I have never been very squeamish, and Sarah is alive—I have all the visual evidence I could ever dream of having. Sarah is alive; she survived her second double lung transplant, and now day by day, minute by minute, we need to survive the next week. Next week, I will look into her eyes, awake and alert, and be able to say, "I love you! You did it! You got lungs! You are going to live!" This image carries me.

# 17. Recovery

The first twenty-four hours are the hardest. Sarah and the new lungs are struggling. Not like last time, but despite being on a ventilator and oxygen, her $O_2$ stats continue to creep lower and lower. You always want 100 percent on the pulse oximeter, but anything in the 90s will suffice. Little by little, Sarah's stats continue to drop, until she is sitting in the upper 80s and her doctors are alarmed. It's not a crisis or a code blue but just the knowledge that we need to do something different; Sarah and her lungs need more time to rest and heal. She needs greater support.

Among the concerns is the possibility of an infection. Could Sarah have an infection in the new lungs? This would be terrible news, as she is completely immunosuppressed, but a very real possibility for someone who has spent so much time open on an operating table. The doctors order an array of broad-spectrum antibiotics, but they will take time to kick in, and Sarah needs help now. The x-rays overall look OK, not perfect, but not bad.

Dr. Spray makes the call that Sarah should be switched to a different type of ventilator, called an oscillator. This enormous machine is quickly wheeled into the room, and a team of respiratory therapists work rapidly to hook and unhook tubing to make a quick and seamless switch from one vent to the next. The oscillator, when up and running, can be heard all the way down the hallway and practically around the corner. It's that loud. *Phish, thump, phish, thump, phish, thump* in rapid unrelenting succession goes the vent.

And even more bizarre than the racket it makes is the way it forces Sarah to breathe. It seems very unnatural, rapid, little fast breaths. How could she possibly be getting any air in before it's forced right back out? It's unlike any ventilator she's ever been on, and we have had some experience. But for all its noise and unnaturalness, it works. Slowly, Sarah's numbers increase, and the sigh of relief is palpable. Disaster, once again, seems to be averted.

Over the past several months, I have learned how to focus on the moment. It's critical to survival here. Don't look back and don't look forward; only look at what's right in front of you. When I catch myself doing either, I intentionally stop myself, but it is hard. If I have to recite a prayer or turn on a TV show to redirect myself, then that's what I do, but I actively try hard to stay in the present mind-set.

Right now, I am washing her little puffy fingers and toes one by one. Putting cream on each one as I finish. Just relishing my beautiful little girl and the fact that she is right here in front of me. I clean and braid her hair and let the past go; this is the moment to live in.

For about three weeks, Sarah has been intubated, sedated, and paralyzed. She does not move at all. The team at CHOP has taught me the importance of us moving and repositioning her body on a schedule, and I help carefully maneuver Sarah into new positions along with her nurse. I want to be a part of every bit of this recovery.

The visual is still tough. Sarah's heart beating so close in such a detailed way; it takes some getting used to, but we do. The film that's covering it is just a little darker than the color of her skin and seems to mold to the surface of her organs, making the details more pronounced. The film clearly has more than one layer, and pools of blood pocket in between these layers. So, in addition to being able to clearly see her heart and lungs working, there are pools of blood on top of them—imagine that.

There is an endotracheal tube down her throat and tape plastered across her face to hold it in position. Respiratory therapists send a smaller tube down the ET periodically to suction secretions out of her new lungs. She still has four thick drainage tubes protruding from her chest with bloody fluid gathering in canisters by the bed. And then there are the tubes sending medication, food, and fluid into her in a constant stream, accompanied by repeated beeping and reloading. Everything is being watched, measured, and recorded. This is a sophisticated dance with a critically ill and fragile child.

Within a couple of days, we are told the good news. Doctors believe Sarah no longer needs the oscillator and can step down to a less invasive ventilator. Apparently, being on the oscillator long term is not good for the lungs; it's a good short-term solution but not a long-term plan. Additionally, the doctors are hoping that with the swelling coming down, they will be able to close her chest. This is exciting news because then we get to wake her up; however, none of this can happen while still dependent on the oscillator.

Sarah successfully switches over to the previous ventilator and holds her stats, and for the first time in a long time, we kind of have the wind in our sails. Bit by bit, little by little, Sarah is surviving her first week, and each day our odds look better and better. Every moment is a victory.

Thankfully, the room once again has nighttime and daytime; lights can be turned on and off, leading to better sleep habits for Fran and me. Sharon left for home once Sarah was stable on the oscillator. We can feel the sense that the crisis is in our rearview mirror. Fran and I get back on strict shifts, only spending a few hours awake and together. It's hard living through the same moment with someone but having to function entirely separately, because even though you are not alone, you really are.

Despite the enormity of what still lies in front of us, our stress levels are much lower than they were just five days ago. Sarah is on the path to recovery, albeit a long one, but at least she is on it. At this point, she is not awake or in pain, so life is calm and routine; there is very little for us to do but wait and watch, and it is a more pleasant kind of waiting than we have had lately. There is the idea that these lungs are working, maybe not perfectly, but a far cry better than her CF lungs. There is this hope for a future now, one without oxygen and machines eventually. There is a realization dawning that maybe, just maybe, she might someday recapture her childhood and be whole again.

In just days we will get to see her again, all of her. It's an anxious, worried, but mostly hopeful waiting. A lot has happened since Sarah was intubated and sedated lying in that PICU, and we won't realize the full impact of that and her recovery until she is awake. There is this lingering fear in me that when she coded, there was a loss of oxygen, but my overwhelming feeling is positive. We are waiting to find out what kind of life she will have—*life*. We are now waiting for her next step in life, rather than her death. It's a much better place to be in, and I can't wait to tell her that she got new lungs.

Just as promised, the one-week mark comes, and they promptly schedule Sarah for a trip to the operating room. It will not be Dr. Spray this time but Dr. Stephanie Fuller. She is an amazing cardiothoracic surgeon, who assisted in one of Sarah's two transplants (for the life of me, I can't remember which one). Periodically, she checks in on Sarah, so she is a very familiar face.

Dr. Fuller is confident that she can close Sarah's chest without trimming the lungs in any way, which is a huge relief. They take her into the OR, and it's quick, no fuss or muss; it's fast. We don't go to the waiting room this time; we just sit in her hospital room and wait because she is going to come right back, and there is not an expectation that she will need a recovery period.

Sarah comes back into the room, still sedated and intubated but put back together again. She has a thick gauze bandage across her chest, so we can't see the wound itself. They have closed her successfully. They have not had to trim the lungs any further, and it is our next victory. They immediately begin the process of weaning her sedation.

It's a slow process over several hours. At first, we notice a rise in her heart rate, a sign that she is more aware of her body and of her discomfort. Next, her fingers move slightly. We can see her stirring a little bit, and eventually she opens her sweet little eyes, immediately searching for me, relief on her face when she sees me by her side. And I know right then and there that my Sarah is not lost to me—those searching eyes know her mom.

Sarah quickly lets me know through hand squeezing and facial expressions that she is very upset about the ET in her mouth going down her throat. It must feel awful. I ask her yes/no questions, and I ask her to squeeze my hand for the responses because she can't speak with the tube.

"Can you hear me? I know you have the tube down your throat. I know you are upset about it."

I can see the anguish in her face. She is clearly in pain, but, yes, she can hear me.

"Sarah, you got lungs. You are going to be OK. I know everything hurts, but you got lungs."

I don't explain everything. A lot has happened, and someday she will learn her story, but today this is all she needs to know.

Sarah is still on tons of heavy sedatives. It's frankly question-able what she is going to remember from this conversation, but this is the mantra I will keep saying until it sticks.

She has severe muscle weakness. The doctors say severe muscle atrophy is a particularly big problem for patients who have spent so much time sedated and paralyzed. It will make the recovery harder. She doesn't have the strength to even lift her arm at this point, just little hand squeezes and nods, but she is clearly com-municating despite her limitations.

It is clear to me that she understands what I am saying, nod-ding from time to time and squeezing my hand with appropriate responses. Most important, though, she knows who I am, she knows who Fran is.

That was always my biggest fear—that she would wake up and be damaged to the point where she didn't know herself or us. I don't for one minute think we have an easy rehab here, but I know immediately that this is my Sarah, unchanged at the essence. She knows who I am, she knows her daddy, she knows where she is, and she understands what happened to her. She is upset about the tube down her throat, and she is in pain. And through the hand squeezing and slight nods of the head, she communicates all of this very well.

So now we start the hard work. We have a huge, hard road ahead of us. Our child's body has been through tremendous trauma. She has been paralyzed and sedated for weeks and is still on a ventilator. She still can't eat by mouth and is getting all her food through IVs. She has four drainage tubes coming out of her chest still, even though the overall chest is closed. The road ahead of us looks more like a mountain, but it's so much better than the alternative. All we have in front of us now is possibility.

This is the greatest moment because she is there, and she has a future, and that is all she wanted. She wanted a chance, and now she has one. I finally have the moment I have dreamed of for so long. This is the kind of fight Sarah can do. She is a tenacious, fierce fighter if given the chance. This is the kind of fight that people with cystic fibrosis spend their whole lives working up to. We have been fighting her whole life for the possibility, for the chance, and now we have it, no matter how hard. This is the beginning of everything.

## Lora

When I first see Sarah after her transplants, I am stunned at how physically debilitated she is. As time goes on and I see how hard she will have to work to get her life back, I find myself even more enraged at UNOS than I was in May and early June when we were fighting the transplant system. I guess I was too overwhelmed by fear before the transplants to feel raw anger. The anger I felt then was more of the righteous indignation type. What I feel now is more like rage.

As I watch Sarah suffering, I am so angry. I can't help but compare Sarah's situation to the transplant recoveries of other CF patients I have seen—people who go into transplant without atrophied muscles or broken backs, people who were walking around—maybe even at home—the day before their transplants.

I think about how Sarah could have been out of bed the day after surgery with an intact spine and well-conditioned muscles if she had received a transplant sooner. Maybe Sarah would never have had to live in the hospital at all had UNOS allowed her an equitable place on the adult waiting list. She should not have had to wait for her parents to take the transplant system to court while she was dying in the PICU.

# 18. Extubation

The work of recovery begins right away—so fast that it surprises me. It's less than twenty-four hours after those sweet eyes opened, and they are ready to get Sarah sitting up and moving as much, or in our case, as little as possible. This is scary and amazing all at once. I am scared for what I know is the inevitable pain, but excited to be working toward something positive finally.

The physical therapist arrives with a lot of help. There is a respiratory therapist, several nurses, and other people whose roles I can't identify. There are a lot of people in the room. Sarah is still attached to dozens of tubes with medication, fluids, and food streaming through them. She has four drainage tubes protruding from her chest and an ET tube down her throat. There is a freshly stitched wound spanning the width of her chest. All these factors make this a slow and strategic dance with a lot of players. Every movement must be extraordinarily gentle and carefully choreographed.

The team plans each person's role and position before they even begin. Sarah looks worried but still can't talk and express her feelings. My heart breaks for her, but I know this is one of many painful things we must work through to get to the other side of transplant. The plan is to get Sarah to sit at the edge of her bed for several minutes; that's it. It doesn't sound like much, but it is an enormous task for a child who has been flat on her back paralyzed and sedated for almost a month.

My role is just emotional support for Sarah, which is good because I don't want to be the one causing her pain. As I watch her struggle painfully to roll to her side (with plenty of assistance) and reach her arm (which is shaking) to the side rail, I experience a tremendous moment of realization of how far she has to go. She tries to give herself a little pull on the side rail, but I can see on her face that it is obvious to her that she has little control over her own body. She almost can't do it at all.

A generous estimate might be that she is able to accomplish 5–10 percent of the work of sitting, using all her force and will, and that this little bit causes her a lot of pain and suffering. Her face is contorted with sadness and pain, but she never quits or tries to stop.

Finally, they get her sitting at the edge of the bed; someone is sitting behind her and someone is spotting the front of her. Using her muscles just to sit is something that she hasn't done in a long time, so they are braced for a fall. The goal is just to sit there at the edge of the bed for just a few minutes, and it's a hard goal for her to reach. The whole experience is eye-opening; we have a tremendously long way to go. I can feel a little panic rising in me. *How will I get her from this place back to childhood?* But I quickly squelch that feeling and get back in the moment. I can't fall apart here; that won't help Sarah. This full realization of the physical impact of the trauma and weeks of sedation she has experienced is a hard pill to swallow.

I am her cheerleader, telling her what a great job she is doing, but the ridiculousness of us being excited about her sitting on the edge of the bed is not lost on her. She is not pleased that being able to do *this* should be an accomplishment, yet it is.

She is exhausted from this activity, very uncomfortable, and in pain, and we lay her back down and try to adjust her back into a comfortable position. The ET is bothering her. It's a very, very thick tube, which gags her with any nudge or shift. And she is struggling to communicate this—and all sorts of other thoughts—to me, but without a voice and little use of her hands, it is mostly a guessing game, which she is too tired and frustrated to play. I can tell she feels trapped inside herself with what must be a million scary thoughts.

Thank God the CICU is prepared for this scenario, and the sweetest child-life specialist comes to the rescue. She is armed with an iPad, which has a special app that we load with pictures so Sarah can start to communicate some of her wants and needs. It's a far cry from being able to talk, but it's something. We quickly learn as she pushes the water button over and over and over with a not very pleased look on her face that her biggest complaint is not being able to drink water.

Unfortunately, this is not a request we can honor, and this frustrates her deeply. The problem is that the ET, which goes down her throat, is basically forcefully holding open the passage between her mouth and her lungs. So, they are very concerned about water getting into the new lungs. All we can offer is a damp, pink sponge which has been sitting in ice, and she can only have one every thirty minutes or so. Because she is so frustrated—angry, really—and groggy on the pain medications, I have to keep re-explaining the reason to her. It's hard to deny her such a seemingly simple request, but the fire in her eyes is further confirmation that my feisty, fierce girl is still there.

Even though her chest has been cut open, and she is very sore, we must do at least mild chest physical therapy—avoiding the wound, of course, but it's nonetheless very painful. We also must suction her lungs through the ET, which furthers that gag reflux. All of this is critical because her ability to cough and clear her own lungs is very compromised by the ET down her throat.

Within a day of waking, the doctors explain to me that it's critical that we wean the ventilator quickly so that she can be extubated—get the ET removed. This is welcome news, but again I am shocked that this is even a possibility after watching her try to get up to a sitting position. They explain that these are *not* CF lungs and that weaning the vent will likely be easier than I expect. Further, apparently, most patients wean their vent within twenty-four hours of transplant. But because of Sarah's extensive trauma, they will stretch the wean over three days, ideally.

If she cannot wean off the vent quickly, she will need to get a tracheostomy, which is something I want to avoid. Long-term ET use is linked to infections, and that's something my immuno-compromised kid cannot risk. I am fully warned and rightfully stressed as we begin the process. There is a certain number they are looking for on the vent, and we all have our eyes on the target. Every few hours the settings are tweaked, and so far, the weaning is going off without a hitch.

In between our weaning vent numbers, which bit by bit re-quires more muscular work of breathing done by Sarah, they are also continuing with all the physical rehab. Each day they are get-ting Sarah to do a little more. The first day, they sat her at the edge of the bed; the second day, they transferred her to a chair; and by the third day, she is out of bed in a chair and painting a picture. Even the act of painting a picture is a struggle. So far, we have not even tried to stand, but the team knows that when the ET comes out, rehab will be much faster and more aggressive; it is holding us back, which is another reason it must come out. I'm still struck by the level of Sarah's disability. Down the road, Dr. McBride (a.k.a. Dr. Mike) will confide to me that she was in one of the worst physical conditions he had ever seen in a post-transplant patient.

Before we know it, Sarah hits the target numbers on the vent, and it is time to extubate. Sarah is nervous but very excited to get the tube out. She is anxious to talk and finally drink fluids. A big team fills the room for this event, which is my first clue that it is possible this could go badly. I guess I thought if she was able to reach the preset vent numbers, all would be well, but looking around her room at all these people, I know this is not a guarantee, and my nerves start to get the best of me.

The doctors are so kind with Sarah. They explain exactly what will happen and wait until she is ready. They let her know that as soon as the ET is out they will place an oxygen mask over her face, so she will not have to do everything herself all at once. They tell her that if this is still not enough, they have a BiPAP machine ready and running, and they will put that on her if she needs it. Finally, they tell her that she is entirely safe as they gesture around the room full of doctors. Sarah nods in understanding, and they pull the tube out.

Immediately, Sarah struggles, and we can see the panic on her face.

"Sarah, it's OK. The doctors say it can take a minute to adjust," I reassure her. "You are safe!"

But my words do little to quell her panic. She seems like she can't get enough air in, and her stats are dropping. It's a very nerve-racking experience. They quickly switch Sarah from plain oxygen to a BiPAP machine, which not only delivers oxygen but also helps with the push-and-pull muscular work of breathing.

The doctors are whispering to each other, and I can tell there is something specific about the way she is breathing that concerns them. Up until this point, I was right in her face encouraging her, but now I look down at her chest and see that it is not natural looking at all. She looks like she is only breathing on one side or sideways. I don't know what to make of it. It looks very odd, and I can tell that everybody in the room is concerned by it. There is clearly a discussion going on that this is a sign of something in particular, but I am trying my best to just focus on Sarah, who is now in full-blown panic.

Remember, this is a kid who has had a lifetime of breathing struggles and has a real fear of death from lack of oxygen. Asking her to be calm while she is struggling to breathe is a monumental request. She is only ten. Her panic is making the situation worse, not better, and I am trying to talk her off the proverbial cliff as her heart races. She starts to speak to me in a scratchy, raw whisper, a little voice I have longed to hear.

"I can't breathe, Mommy! Help!"

"It's OK, Sarah. I know this is upsetting, but you are OK. These doctors are not going to let anything bad happen. They need you to try for a little longer."

Sarah vigorously shakes her head no, eyes wide, heart racing, and I want someone to jump in and help. I repeat to the doctors that she feels like she can't breathe. And they acknowledge that something appears to be wrong but that they need her to try for a little longer. They reiterate that she is safe. I am so upset for her; she is clearly terrified, and I feel helpless. But what does this mean?

After what feels like an eternity but is only about twenty minutes, they decide that she needs to be re-intubated. Quickly, they shoot sedation through her IV, and within a minute or two, she is re-intubated and stabilized.

## Sarah

When I first wake up, my mind is so cloudy, and I really just want to fall back asleep. Mommy is talking to me, but I'm not focusing or paying attention to anything. I am really, really thirsty, and I keep trying to tell everyone, but no one understands me, because I have this dang tube down my throat.

So, they give me an iPad with pictures, since I can't talk. If you click on the picture, it will say the word for you. Water is my favorite icon. But still no one ever brings me water. Instead they bring me this dumb, little pink sponge on a stick. They dab it in ice chips, with I guess some water, and hand it to me. They think *that* will solve my problem? And I'm thinking, *Um, yay, no.* So I keep banging on that icon, being like, *I'm thirsty still.* Then I have to wait forever, I swear, an hour or more, before another little, dumb sponge appears. I am so mad about that sponge. I never want to see another little pink sponge in my life.

Then like twelve people come in the room to help me sit up in bed, and it is very painful, and I can't really even move my hand or anything. I can't move much at all. But I'm tired and I just want to go back to sleep. I am not thinking clearly; everything is a blur.

My first real detailed memory is when they take the tube out of my throat. A lot of people are in the room again, and they tell me they are going to take out the tube. I am like, *Oh my God, yes!* (but in my head since I can't talk). So, they take it out, and it is a little weird at first, but I try to relax. Right away, though, I have trouble breathing without the tube. I start to get very upset, panic, in my head. It is really hard for me to breathe. It is very stressful, because you need to breathe to live. I don't necessarily think I am going to die, but I am scared.

They tell me to relax, to keep trying. I think, *Are these people crazy? They want me to keep trying again and again after this is clearly not a success.* And you know it's bad, because I want that dang tube back down my throat. Even though I hate the tube, I despise the tube, I hate the tube in every way, at least I can breathe with it.

Mommy is right in my face saying, "It's going to be OK. Everything is fine."

And I think, *Oh my God, are you crazy, woman? Everything's not fine. It's not OK. It's clearly not OK, Mom. Can't you see that it's not OK? You kept telling me it's fine, but it's not fine.*

Then, finally, they decide to put the tube back, and I go to sleep.

# 19. Tracheostomy

Sarah is sedated, comfortable, and breathing with the aid of the ET again, while doctors begin to explain the problem. The sideways, or one-sided, look of her breathing is a very specific indicator, and it tells them there is nerve damage affecting the right diaphragm, that her right diaphragm is permanently paralyzed. It is not an unusual complication, but it means that Sarah needs a tracheostomy, and I feel very defeated by this news.

I want Sarah to have a typical life and childhood, unattached to machines. While I was very prepared for a slow physical rehab, I felt confident that soon she would be free of machines for breathing. For eighteen months now, Sarah has lived a very separate life from her peers, and I want normalcy for her.

But the hits keep coming. The doctors explain that Sarah will now need several more surgeries, and I look at my weak, sleeping child, and I think, *How will we ever overcome?* I just want no one to touch her ever again. I am done with the torture and the pain. I finally have her back, and with each trip back to that OR, there is a risk that my heart can no longer bear. But, alas, there is no choice. We must move forward; we must move through this. There is no path to the place we want to be that doesn't travel through immense pain and suffering.

In the first surgery, they will reopen the transplant incision on the right side to give them access to the right diaphragm. Doctors will then permanently tie down the paralyzed section, because right now it is floating and preventing the right lung from properly inflating. She will then be able to recover for forty-eight hours before being brought back into the OR again for the tracheostomy.

"Why can't you do both surgeries at once? Now that we have decided she needs a trach, I would rather hurry up and get there," I explain.

"Sarah's not strong enough to risk that amount of time in the OR and physical trauma all at once," explains the attending.

My poor baby. My heart just breaks for her. It's this long and drawn-out thing, and it's so upsetting. I just want one thing to go right, one thing to be easy for her.

In between all these surgeries, we continue to physically rehab her as much as her body will allow. The trauma lying ahead is unbearable to me. She is ten; my heart breaks.

But wait—there is more. Because Sarah has been accepting limited food into her stomach via a feeding tube called a G-tube for months now, we need to begin the process of slowly getting her gut up and working again. We cannot transition her medications from IV to oral unless that stomach is working, of course, and the doctors would like to begin that process now. As part of this, they want a new kind of feeding tube in place. It's called a J-G tube. Simply explained, they want to use the existing incision of her G-tube and thread a different type of tube into place.

It's not complicated but must be done under certain guided technology in the interventional radiology (IR) department. The good news, I think, is there will be no need for sedation or further cutting. The bad news is my little girl, who is terrified at this point, needs to undergo another procedure. So, when the doctors in IR arrive with their consent forms, I am in a particularly special state of mind.

"So, we just need you to sign here and here. We should be able to fit Sarah into the schedule tomorrow," says Dr. Unknown, who is about to have the "pleasure" of dealing with me.

"She will not be sedated, correct?" I ask.

"That's right. There's no need for sedation since there will be no new incision," he explains, clearly pleased to be sharing the good news.

"Then I will be going back with her," I say confidently.

"Uh, no, we have a policy of no parents in IR," he says firmly.

"Well, that's a problem, because I have a policy of my un-sedated child having her mother with her for procedures. So, I guess IR's policy and my policy don't match. Therefore, I can't sign consent." I say this with a deadpan calm, because of all the things that have rattled me this week, Dr. Unknown will not be one of them.

"But she must go back; otherwise, they cannot deliver her medication to her," he explains, believing logic and common sense are on his side.

"Nah, they can keep putting them through her veins. In fact, look at her, she's getting meds right now."

Now he is incredulous. "She can't do it that way forever," he says as if I am just that dumb.

But, honestly, I have been brought to the brink of crazy, and I don't even blink as I say in total calm, "I guess she's going to have to, seeing as IR's policy and my policy don't match. My policy is either sedation alone or not sedated with mom, and I'm certainly not changing my policy."

"Well, we are not doing either of those things," he says with just the most priceless astounded look on his face.

"Okay, that's fine, then I will not be able to sign consent." And

I turn and walk back over to Sarah, signaling that our conversation is over.

But Dr. Unknown is naive and young and has not met anyone quite as unreasonable as I am, and he still believes deep in his heart that I can be convinced.

"We never have parents in IR. It's like taking you back to the OR while we are operating."

"I understand. It was nice meeting you," I say.

He is irritated with me, just completely exasperated. "But your kid needs this."

"I know. Well, I guess my kid's just not going to get it," I calmly reply. And he finally leaves, but I know I have not heard the last of this. They know that they cannot do this without my permission, and sitting by my child in IR is not a big thing to ask for at this point.

A little time passes, and poor Dr. Goldfarb comes into the room. It's not his usual time for rounds, so I know he is the one who has been sent to talk reason into me.

"So, I hear you won't sign consent for Sarah to go back to IR?" he says.

"Yup, that's right," I say.

"It's not a big deal. She won't be in any pain. They will take very good care of her."

"I understand, but if she is awake, I am going, too, or she is not going. It's as simple as that."

Unlike Dr. Unknown, Dr. Goldfarb knows me quite well. He knows that I don't even leave Sarah's hospital room when any other reasonable parent would, so I can see on his face that he totally recognizes this is an uphill battle and one that he will probably lose.

I'm not sure what Dr. Goldfarb goes back and tells them, but he does not push me any further on the issue. I imagine it goes something like this: "Listen, she's crazy, and if she says she won't send her back, she won't. I'd like to help you, but there's nothing I can do, so can we all just let her go back so that I can move on from this?"

Anyway, later that day, it is agreed that I will go back with Sarah, and I sign consent.

So, it is a week of stress, and it's a new kind of stress from what we have been dealing with in the very recent past. We have been dealing with the stress of dying before this, which is obviously the most awful kind of stress. But now we are dealing with the stress of a ten-year-old going through tremendous pain and suffering, and that is a new kind of awful. This is hard.

At this point, I suspect Sarah is depressed, but I don't know because she cannot speak to me. I imagine she feels like she waited for this big thing to happen and her life is not better; it's pretty bad. There hasn't been this big, amazing moment where she takes a breath with her new lungs and can see that it will all be worth it. Instead, she tried to breathe, and the reality was terrifying. And I have to say, if I were the patient going through all this, I would be terrible. She is in pain and uncomfortable, and although she complains in her own way (even though she still can't speak), she does everything asked of her. She does not resist doing the work of recovery.

Each trip to the operating room will be traumatic. Sarah has a tremendous fear of dying, for good reason. She is now very scared once again that she has lungs that do not work.

All she has to go on is blind faith that we know what we are doing.

So, they take her back for the first in the series of surgeries; the diaphragm plication, which seems to go smoothly. Next, IR for the G-J tube, and I sit by her side the whole time. And finally, we are preparing to go back for the trach. I have tried to explain it to her, but she is very groggy, and I am not sure she understands. I try to focus her on the tube down her throat going away.

This is the surgery that I am most worried about, because nothing about it is temporary. This will be her new way of life for some time, and I have no idea what to expect. Will it hurt? Will it feel weird to eat and talk with a trach? It's such a big and permanent thing, and I'm afraid of what that will be like for her. I have very little knowledge or experience with trachs, and the unknown is frightening.

I anxiously watch Sarah as she begins to wake from the tracheostomy. It's nice to see her face without all the tubes and tape, and I couldn't be more surprised than when she wakes up totally happy. The trach turns out to be the best thing, and if I could go back, I wouldn't have worried so much or pushed back as much. She wakes up from this surgery immediately feeling better. She no longer has that feeling of having something down her throat. She can speak, and shortly after surgery, she can drink, too. These little pieces change the whole experience in our room. Sarah is happy!

This is a turning point in her recovery. Her physical therapy starts to gain momentum because she is not hindered by the uncomfortable ET, which required us to move slowly and carefully. She can communicate any of her fears, while before she was trapped inside herself. And being able to drink water is huge for her. It was driving her insane not to be able to drink.

Quickly after this, her chest tubes begin to slow down on the drainage, and one by one they get removed. It's the weirdest thing to me; with Sarah just sitting there in bed, they pull the tubes right out of her. In the operating room, they already threaded the stitches in place, so now they just pull the tube out and pull the stitch to close the hole.

Sarah's a pretty tough kid. She doesn't get upset about this. She just says it feels weird.

## Sarah

I am scared to go back into the operating room, but I still can't speak and explain my feelings to anyone. Mom knows I'm scared, but there is little she can do to make it better. I am so sleepy that I guess I don't really understand what any of the operations are about. Mom tries to explain it, but I am not really following it.

But when I wake up, I am surprised at how good I feel. The tube is gone! I can talk! I can drink! And I actually feel good.

My voice is very weak at first, kind of like a whisper, but I have a voice. The tube felt so uncomfortable, but with the trach I don't feel anything. It is such a relief. The trach doesn't feel like much of anything to me. I am happy.

# 20. The Media

It has been about two weeks since Sarah's first transplant and still almost no one knows that it failed. I have been unusually silent on social media, and people are speculating that something is wrong. It is time that we share the painful truth of her second transplant and all the hardship that has followed, but I haven't even told my friends and family, nonetheless the world.

I know I did what I needed to do to survive personally. I thought Sarah was dying, and I was not prepared to live through that publicly, but now so much has changed. There will never be a good time for me to walk away from Sarah, to share this news, but I know I need to do it soon. I cannot let any more time pass. If I wait any longer, I know the truth will leak out anyway, and that's not how I want Sarah's story told.

My sisters tell my dad and the rest of our immediate family, who seem relieved to have been spared the trauma of living through this with us. Fran tells his parents. I tell Maureen and Tracy myself. I guess I should feel some remorse for not including everyone who loves and worked so hard to save Sarah, but I don't because my emotions are so overwhelmingly about Sarah that it's hard to see anything else. It wasn't something I did to shut people out; it's what I did to survive.

Maureen and Tracy are very kind to me but are clearly shocked that I kept such an enormous thing from them, especially after everything they had done. After telling them, I start to worry that I may have put them in a bad position. They had been updating the media diligently, and I just dropped out of communication, leaving them hanging. The whole time I was so overwhelmed with my own personal nightmare that I never thought of anything outside Sarah's room. I can tell they are worried that I did the wrong thing keeping this a secret. I get their point. From a strategic standpoint, they are right. However, I was capable of nothing more than surviving. This is my only defense. I survived; that's it. Once they learn everything that's happened, they totally get it but strongly believe we need to get out there quickly and honestly open up about why I was silent.

I am also worried that the public will feel betrayed because of my silence, which was never my intention. And now, since talking to Tracy and Maureen, I worry the media will feel deceived or misled because I kept this secret. Before this moment, I did not spend any time worrying about the public and the media because I saw this from such a different perspective; my kid was dying. I could manage nothing but my own emotions. But now, as I am preparing to head to the curb outside CHOP to give this update, I am scared. I can see this from a different perspective now, and I fear no one will be able to see it from mine. There was no other way for me to manage what I had managed. Emotionally, I had nothing to give anyone but Sarah until this moment. But can I make them see that?

## Maureen Garrity

The night of the first transplant, Tracy and I leave the hospital to give Sarah's family private time. We know the next few days will be critical and that we will need to give them a couple of days before checking in to see how things are coming along. Our job now will be to provide updates to the press when we get them but also to try to slow down the media circus a bit if we can—for the sake of the family.

What we don't anticipate is the deafening silence that follows—with almost no communication from Janet and Fran about how Sarah is doing. In our hearts, we fear the worst. Maybe something has gone terribly wrong. It is an uncomfortable time for Team Sarah. We have been there day and night for the past month, and we care deeply about Sarah and her family. And the media has, understandably, become accustomed to round-the-clock updates and access to the family and us. Now they are going without information. Without anything to report, we worry the media will feel used by the family and us and will turn negative. Luckily, most are understanding, but we can tell they are frustrated, as we are.

It is close to two weeks after the first surgery when we find out from Janet what happened the night of Sarah's transplant: that Sarah coded; that her new lungs were too damaged to work; that the doctors put Sarah immediately on something called ECMO in the hopes they could find another set of lungs to save her; and that their wish had come true with a second set of lungs three days later.

When Tracy and I learn what happened, we immediately understand why Janet and Fran have not been communicating with us or the media. Up to the day of Sarah's June 12 lung transplant, we were amazed at how strong they had been. But after Sarah coded, the family was in too much pain to share outside of those four walls anymore. They were not able to think about the media, their friends, or anyone outside their immediate family. In fact, even most of their immediate family does not know about what happened after the first transplant or that there was a second transplant. Sarah's grandparents do not even know. Janet tells us they had been preparing to say good-bye to Sarah and needed to do this on their own, in their own way.

We decide to hold a press conference to announce what happened. This seems only fair considering the overwhelming support Sarah has received from strangers who have followed her story religiously. Many of these strangers are wonderful members of the media, who we were in touch with daily prior to Sarah's transplant. Without the help of the public and the media, I doubt the federal policy would have been overturned or that anyone would have paid attention to this law at all. These people are heroes of Sarah and her family, and we need to share the story with them. We also prepare for backlash from the public. Why should Sarah have been given a second chance? Was this favoritism? The answer was, "No!" Even after her first transplant failed, Sarah was still the sickest person—child or adult—on the waiting list, and UNOS evaluated her condition and relisted her. Her doctors still felt they could save her, and they did.

As I take a quick look at myself in the mirror before heading out to face the press, I see a person I barely recognize looking back at me. I am a mess. I have not showered in days. My hair is frizzy and clipped haphazardly to the side of my head. One of the few clean shirts I have is stained. Frantically I try to improve the situation by applying a little makeup. Maybe I should take a quick shower before heading out? No, that's too much time away from Sarah; this will have to do.

Walking outside, the sun is bright, such a contrast to my life lived indoors. I can see right away that this is a big deal. There is a large crowd of media stationed across the street, and my stomach does somersaults. I think of the first family who sacrificed to give Sarah life. I pray that if they are watching, if they realize through timing and media reports that they are Sarah's donor, that they will understand me correctly when I speak today.

The failure of the first transplant in no way diminishes their gift. Even though those lungs only lived in Sarah for three days, I strongly believe they saved her life. Sarah was dying. We had very little time. We would not have taken any further extraordinary measures to save her life at that point. We would have let her go peacefully. Because of that first donor, Sarah is alive! When those lungs failed, the doctors knew we needed to try to save their beautiful gift, so emergency measures were taken. Sarah was put on VA ECMO, which allowed her to live long enough to receive the second gift of life. I wish I could tell them this.

I am not sure what Maureen and Tracy have told the media. I know they explained everything to me, but I am scattered, with a million thoughts running through my head. I want people to understand me today, to know my intentions.

As I step up to the cluster of microphones and reporters, I begin to try to explain the moments after transplant. How things turned that night after we had publicly celebrated.

"They called a code blue to her room. We ran down the hallway and found out that her lungs, for whatever reason, were going into a rapid decline," I explained.

I told them that the doctors became quickly clear that there was no chance for these lungs.

"We were told there was a one-in-a-million chance she would live on the current lungs that she had. So, we did not feel like there was a lot of decisions to make there. It was all scary, but it seemed very clear that we needed to go ahead and take this risk."

So, we listed for another set of lungs.

"This all happened very fast, and we were not expecting it. And frankly, we were told in those three days that she was going to die. And so, it was never something that we wanted to keep a secret for any period of time, but it was something that we felt like in that moment we weren't prepared to live out her dying in public.

"So many people have come out, and poured out, and have loved my kid. And it's been the most beautiful thing."

I just wanted people to know that we appreciate them. We did not take all that the public and the media had done for granted. We just were barely surviving.

"Sarah's a fighter; she's always been a fighter. Sarah's not giving up. Sarah's a feisty kid, and she's going to fight through it. And I think this has been harder than Sarah expected. It's been harder than I expected, and that part's been a little depressing, but by no means has Sarah given up."

At the end, I feel good. I think I truly and honestly explained myself. Maureen and Tracy think so, too.

The press does not receive it badly. They get it. I think because I go out there and explain it: my kid was dying, and I wasn't prepared to live that out with you guys. Everyone seems to understand that it was not my intention to deceive anybody. The few critics I have, have always been my critics and always will be. I have learned that much. But the true humanity of people, the love and support, the kindness of the press, there are more good, kind, caring people out there than not.

# 21. Back to the PICU

Finally, it feels like we might be in for some smooth sailing. All the surgeries are finished, and Sarah's physical therapy is moving along at a much more rapid pace. We are getting into a good rhythm, and I finally feel like I can breathe again. But then Dr. Goldfarb comes with news.

"We are going to transfer Sarah back to the PICU," he says casually, clearly not anticipating resistance.

And I know I am supposed to receive this as good news. It means that my child, who has been on bypass twice, on VA ECMO for three days (putting tremendous strain on her heart), is in good cardiac condition. Sarah's heart has rebounded from all the trauma. And while she still needs intensive care, she no longer needs critical support for her heart. So, in the big picture, it says great things about Sarah's condition.

But for me, the PICU has a lot of bad memories. Sarah was dying the last time we were there. I have serious trepidations about going back now that I am accustomed to the people in the CICU, who are all phenomenal. Fran and I have found the staff in the CICU very welcoming; we feel safe and have gotten into a good rhythm here. Why rock the boat? Furthermore, the few bad nursing experiences I have ever had at this hospital have all been in the PICU.

"I really don't want to go back there. Sarah is getting such good care here. Is there any way we can stay? Please let us stay," I say nervously. "Let us stay here until she is well enough to go back to 8-South."

I can see that Dr. Goldfarb is surprised, and he explains that the CICU has a very limited number of beds and patients just cannot stay once their hearts no longer pose a risk.

Within twenty-four hours, Sarah's transfer is under way. The PICU is an enormous department, and I'm relieved to see we are nowhere near the "room of death" that she barely survived.

All the focus is now on Sarah's physical rehabilitation. All day long, a stream of doctors and therapists comes in and out of our room with the sole focus of physical rehab. Everyone wants Sarah up and moving. In the morning, an occupational therapist (OT) arrives and works on Sarah's personal skills, with a focus on fine-motor skills—brushing her teeth, combing her hair, buttoning her shirt. The OT gets Sarah up and moving each day, even though Sarah tries to convince him that the day starts at noon and not at 9:00 A.M.

Next, a speech pathologist comes in to work with Sarah on swallowing soft foods. Sarah has not eaten by mouth in months, and they need to make sure she can do this safely since getting the tracheostomy before they can clear her to eat solid food. They slowly work their way up to more solid foods. The speech therapist also works with Sarah on being able to project her voice, which is still very raspy and soft.

Dr. Mike brings the big guns—weights. He has arm weights and leg weights. Getting her muscles back in shape is critical to her rehab. As she does repetition after repetition—as slowly as she can get away with—she rolls her eyes at him. This is her least favorite type of rehab, and she is so sleepy from the narcotic pain medication she is on that at times she looks like she might nod off.

Finally, we have PT coming. Their job is to get Sarah standing and walking again. This is no small task and probably the hardest thing anyone expects her to do but also the most gratifying, because each day she gets closer and closer to physical independence.

There is a whole big world opening to Sarah as we progress with each of these skills. It is a different feeling from the rehab we were doing before transplant, which felt like torture with the possibility of no eventual payoff. Then, we questioned how much we should push her, because it didn't feel right to put her through so much pain if she was going to die. Now, we know the rehab is her gateway to a new life—and that she has everything she needs now to have a life. It is just a matter of pushing through this to something better. So even though it is very hard, it is also very gratifying because she starts to get results.

About a week into our stay in the PICU, Sarah's physical therapist, Rebecca, gets Sarah to the edge of her bed and into a chair, and Sarah pulls herself into a standing position unassisted while holding on to her walker. She is standing without anyone helping her. This is a huge milestone. Just over a week previously, we were cheering when she sat at the edge of her bed with massive assistance. Today she is standing using her own muscle and willpower. It's very exciting.

The rehabilitation process is very tedious, but it is also much easier to push her now that the ET is gone and the chest tubes have been removed. In the beginning, Sarah can't do the most basic physical tasks, but it is very rewarding because we can see an independent child emerging bit by bit. The progress may be slow, but it is steady.

The heavy narcotics she still requires are a thorn in our side, though. The doctors are trying to balance pain management with the need for Sarah to be alert. Sarah says that when she looks back on this time, her memory is a bit scattered because of the narcotics she was on.

And despite all the pain meds, she is in a lot of pain. Most of this pain is in her back, where she has those compression fractures. The wound on her chest is not fully healed, but she never complains about it. The back pain, though, overwhelms everything. The doctors tell us that they would usually brace a child with this type of fracture to support the spine and help with the discomfort, but they are afraid a brace would put too much pressure on her new lungs. So, we are stuck.

Even with these challenges, little by little she starts to be able to do more and more. Now Sarah is taking steps with the walker. In the morning, she gets up with her OT and goes to the bathroom to brush her teeth rather than practicing those skills in bed. And I start seeing that there could be a light at the end of the tunnel, that we could go home from this.

There is also a more silent rehab Sarah is doing every time her vent settings are adjusted. She is building the muscles to breathe again unassisted, something most of us take for granted. The respiratory therapist continually lowers Sarah's vent settings bit by bit so that she is doing more of the work of breathing than the vent each day.

We are also trying to get a handle on Sarah's hearing loss. She now has hearing aids, and they are helping. We go for a more detailed hearing test and are disturbed to find there is even more damage to her hearing than before. There is nothing we can do; this damage is permanent, and we are beginning to worry that it may be progressive.

All this is the putting back together of Sarah. It is the good work of transplant. Everyone told us the hard work begins after transplant, but to me the hard part was waiting, not knowing if she would ever get a transplant. This work is very satisfying and gratifying, even though it is also a bit of torture because of how debilitated Sarah had become. We are working toward getting back to *life*, which is clearly on the horizon.

While in the past I had told myself to live in the moment, to only think about the moment and not look ahead, at this point whenever she is having a tough time, I paint a picture for her of what this will give her, what she is trying to regain. What our goal is. We are looking ahead more because there are things to look ahead *to*—there are great things to look ahead to.

## Sarah

I don't like the rehab—any of it. Everything seems much harder than I expected. I am still very, very tired; Mom says it's because of the medication I am on. I am in pain. My back is just awful, shooting pains.

Mom says I am a fighter, that I can do this. I am a fighter, but I would like to fight without weights in my hand and pain down my back. I want to sleep in and watch movies and just get better.

Of all the things I can't do—and there are a lot of them—I am most upset by how much trouble I am having talking. I get out of breath when I talk for just a few minutes, and even when I can talk, it is a whisper. More than anything, this is upsetting and frustrating to me. I like to talk all the time, and now I just can't.

I find lifting weights with Dr. Mike exhausting. I can barely sit at the edge of my bed. How can he expect me to lift weights in this circumstance? I don't appreciate standing up. I know everyone is excited for me, but really, let's think about this: we are excited that I can stand. I hate it all, but I know I have to do it; I accept that fact, so I do it but not happily. It's all too hard and hurts too much.

For some reason, I am not worried that I will not walk again or do typical stuff, but I can tell it's a long, long way off, and it's hard to stay positive. It's hard to stay happy when the simplest things are impossible. I wish there were a way I could just skip all of this but still eventually be able to do it all. Sadly, that's not how it works.

# 22. Sarah's Eleventh Birthday

It's August now, about six weeks since transplant and just days from Sarah's eleventh birthday—a birthday that just weeks ago seemed impossible. We have asked to use the nearest playroom for a family party, and Sarah and I now fill our time in between rehab appointments planning a celebration. Fran has returned home to our other children.

"Mommy, I want to give goodie bags to all my cousins," she says as she excitedly surfs the internet for trinkets.

It is the first time in a long time that we are focusing on typical childhood, and I am excited.

"Oh, let's use beach buckets instead of bags, Mom. It's summer, right?"

"That's a great idea," I say as she pops copious amounts of junk in my virtual shopping cart. She is all lit up with excitement.

"Slinkies—everyone likes them—and these ones are like a rainbow. Stuffed animals, glow sticks . . . Mom there's so much good stuff here. How will we choose? How much can I spend?"

At this point, I think she could get away with anything, and I have a sinking suspicion that she knows it, too.

Her big birthday goal is to walk herself all the way to the play-room for the party, with only her walker for assistance. I worry she will tire herself out right before the celebration, but I know this is a good goal, so I say nothing.

I have tasked Fran and Sharon with preparing our kids for the differences they will see in their sister and cousin. I don't think Sarah is that aware of her physical changes since transplant, and I don't want any of the kids inadvertently shining a light on these temporary changes.

Because of Sarah's weak immune system, she has not seen any of her siblings or cousins since Memorial Day weekend and that fateful PICU send-off party. Sarah looks quite different from the tiny, frail little girl the kids last saw months ago. The team has been feeding Sarah aggressively, initially via IV and now through her feeding tube. This, combined with the extraordinarily high doses of prednisone she is on to ward off organ rejection, has caused her to double in size. Additionally, she has the tracheos-tomy, which none of my kids have any experience with, and her voice is still raspy and soft. She is in a much better place overall, and it is exciting to me that she has come so far, but I know the differences in Sarah will be shocking to her siblings, who haven't seen her in so long.

It is a uniquely exciting moment as Sarah carefully walks her-self to the playroom for this special reunion. It's a big moment for me, too. I have not seen my other children in quite some time to avoid the risk of bringing germs back and forth to Sarah and her compromised immune system. We have set up a comfortable rocking chair in the center of the celebration where Sarah will sit.

Sarah's sister, Ella, and brothers, Sean and Finn, are there with her dad. My sisters Sharon and Lora and my brother-in-law, Andy, are also there with their kids, and both sets of grandparents are there. All said, it's a big group, and peppered throughout are many of Sarah's favorite doctors and nurses who continually stop by for visits.

It's overwhelming for me, especially with Sean. He's overly excited and very focused on my attention, emotional, high-strung. It's moments like these where I feel all that mommy guilt for my extended absence. Finn seems fine, almost too fine, disconnected from me, and I worry I've somehow damaged our bond. Ella, on the other hand, is laser focused on Sarah and getting all of Sarah's attention. She does not leave her side for a single second. At the end of the party, Fran brings our kids back to Sarah's room for some extra time with just the six of us. It's nice to be together as a family again finally, but Ella and Sean have a tremendously hard time leaving with Fran at the end. "We are almost there," I promise them.

This is our first real celebration of Sarah's gift of life. Up until now, we have just been surviving. The kids do crafts, play games, and make a lot of noise. At this moment, I feel like we are getting there, back to life and to family. Sarah is eleven, a milestone we were afraid she wouldn't reach, and I can see that we are getting her back little by little.

This day is a highlight in our journey. Yes, Sarah still has significant back pain and is on a tremendous number of painkillers and she is physically uncomfortable throughout the celebration, but she never lets that dim her day. Everything is not perfect in any way, but it is perfect enough for us. We have a great party.

### Sarah

I am so excited to see everyone that I am counting down the days. Mom and I have been planning for this all week. I know the exact room where the party will be because each day for rehab I practice walking the halls, and I head straight there. It's a little playroom place. They have them on 8-South, too, but none of the CF kids are allowed to go in, because kids with CF cannot be near each other. The bad bacteria, like the MAI that led to my transplant, can be transferred from one patient to another. It's a sad, and isolating, part of CF. So, this is the first time I will get to use a CHOP playroom.

My favorite part of planning is making these little buckets with lots of fun stuff—Slinkies, glow sticks, blinky balls. I got so much stuff, I was afraid I would not be able to fit it all in each person's bucket when the time came. Luckily, I figured it out.

Everyone is all very excited when I walk into the room. They are so excited that I think I forgot how loud it was with so many kids around. Ella sits right next to me the whole time, and the boys run around a lot. I get a bunch of presents. One of my favorite presents is a big metal pig statue. Even people who followed my story on TV sent me presents—I can't believe that.

Mom and I planned crafts, so everyone paints these wooden animals at the table. I just feel so happy because I am able to have a birthday party with my family just like I would have if I were at home.

The weeks following this are focused on our one goal—going home. We are in a step-down unit at this point called the PCU. Sarah's come a long way; she can walk small distances unassisted with her walker, and she's eating small amounts of solid food and taking all her medication orally. She is not on many IVs. We are weaning the settings on her vent. All things that point to our approaching homecoming. It's very exciting.

In the PCU, their goal is to prepare us to go home, and that doesn't just mean Sarah hitting certain goals. Fran and I need to learn and prove a few things ourselves. The hospital does one-on-one training for us on Sarah's tracheostomy, cleaning and caring for it, safely changing the tubing, and frighteningly detailed cardiopulmonary resuscitation (CPR). There's nothing like learning to use a resuscitation bag and do CPR on a dummy that you know represents your child and the reality that this skill could be necessary. It's not just training, though. We must put this training into real practice and prove many times on Sarah that we can do all her care before we can leave. It's nerve-racking but clearly totally necessary.

As we have begun to plot her homecoming, I have been pushy with my goals. I know this is shocking; I have a lot of specific opinions. I think, I hope, that Dr. Goldfarb is used to this by now. He must deal with annoying parents all the time. I tell myself that he appreciates this side of me, which is funny if you think about it. I can rationalize anything.

First, I want to leave by the end of August. I am convinced that Sarah will heal better at home and that there is nothing they are doing for her here at this point that I cannot do myself at home. In general, I am pretty cocky about my ability to care for Sarah on my own—a little gutsy, in fact. Maybe more so than I ought to be.

Before transplant, I stayed home way beyond when most people would have thought it reasonable. Sarah was on eight liters of $O_2$ at home and BiPAP more than half the time before I was convinced that we needed to live at CHOP. Home care would meet me at CHOP for my outpatient visits to exchange oxygen tanks because there was not a safe way for me to travel with the amount of $O_2$ necessary for a two-way trip. So, I am a little crazy. And I did this with no nursing help, even though we completely qualified for it.

From the time that Sarah was a baby, I promised myself that we would make CF fit into our life as opposed to making our life fit into CF. I put tremendous pressure on myself for Sarah to have as much normalcy as I could provide in any situation.

So, I push Dr. Goldfarb to pick a date with me.

"I want to leave at the end of August," I say. "It will give Sarah time to be with her siblings before they go back to school, and Sarah and I need to go home."

"I think she should go home when she can walk out of here," says Dr. Goldfarb.

"Oh my God, you have not seen her in rehab. That's going to take forever. You've gotta let me go home before that."

"Well, maybe you guys should go to an inpatient rehab before home," he says.

"No, no, no! I'm going from the hospital to home."

"I'm concerned that you are putting too much on yourself," he explains.

"I will come in every day to see whoever we need to see at CHOP for outpatient rehab," I beg. "I need to get back to my other children; Sarah needs to get back to life. She will rehab faster trying to keep up with her siblings," I rationalize.

I am very pushy, and he and I debate, and it's not what he wants us to do. But at the end of the day, even though I know I am a pain, Dr. Goldfarb trusts me.

"We can set a date for the end of August on one condition. You must have full-time nursing care set up," he says firmly.

"I don't want nursing care. I just want to be a little family again," I say.

"Well, that's the only scenario I will discharge her into at the end of August. Otherwise, you can stay here or go to a rehab facility."

So, I agree, and we set August 27, 2013, as our homecoming date. Dr. Goldfarb is clear that he thinks I am taking on too much. He thinks I would be better off staying a few more weeks and then going to rehab following that, but he knows I would never do anything to compromise Sarah. So, he agrees to let us go, because he knows if I get home and it is too much, I will come back. I have

Fran and me with Sarah just after her first birthday before the CF diagnosis.

Sarah at three doing her twice-a-day nebulizer and vest treatment.

(above) The three best friends: Robby (two-years-old), Sarah (three-years-old), and Jack (one-year-old) together at home.

(left) Sarah during her ballet production at four-years-old.

Fran and me with Sarah at her prekindergarten graduation.

(above) Family vacation at the Jersey Shore: Robby (four), Sarah (five), Sean (two), and Jack (three).

(right) Sarah and her brother Sean, just after Sarah went on full-time oxygen and was listed for transplant.

(above) Pa and Sarah snuggling. We had just learned she had cystic fibrosis–related diabetes.

(opposite top) Weekend family time at the hospital during Sarah's long admission leading to transplant.

(opposite bottom) The day the CHOP chef came to make cake pops with Sarah.

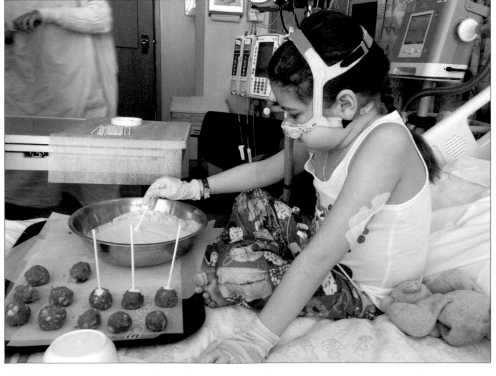

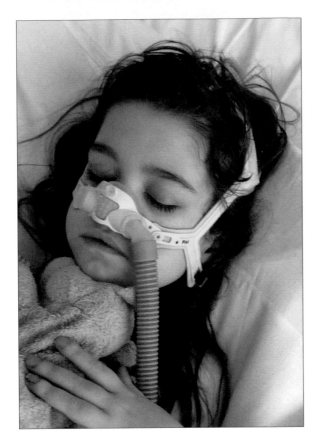

(left) Sarah, now in the PICU, sleeping deeply in the final weeks before transplant.

(below) Sarah after the successful second transplant with the chest closed.

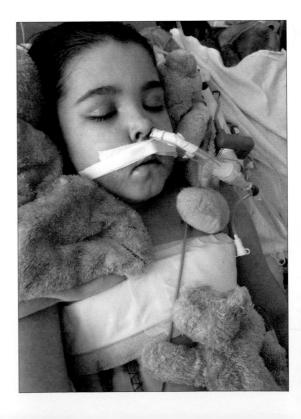

(opposite top) Sarah visiting with her dog, Oreo, at the hospital.

(opposite bottom) The paper lanterns and memory chain decorating Sarah's room at CHOP.

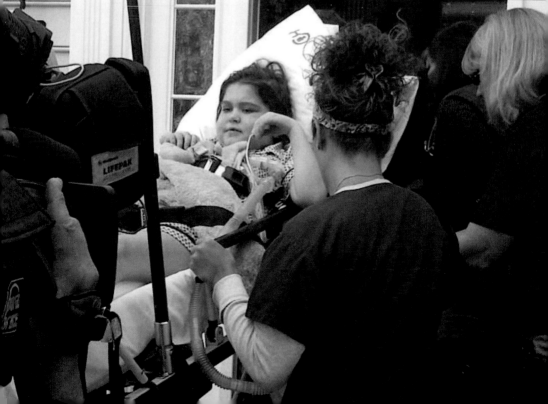

(opposite top) Sarah with some of her cousins at her eleventh birthday party at CHOP.

(opposite bottom) Sarah being wheeled into our home from the ambulance on homecoming day.

(above) Sarah and her cousins playing in the snow, while Sarah practices being off the ventilator.

(right) Sarah and Dr. Mike in rehab.

All of the cousins together, shortly before Sarah's tracheostomy is removed.

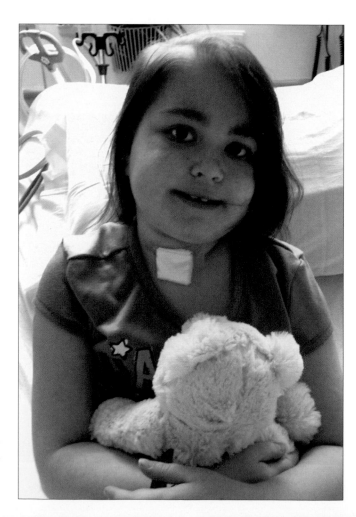

Sarah's one-year transplant anniversary and the day she got the tracheostomy removed.

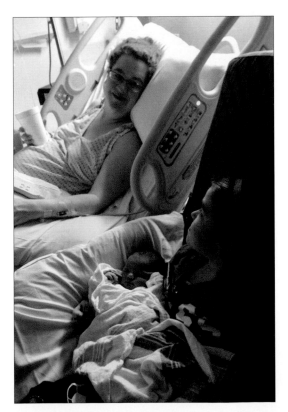

(above) Sarah and siblings joining the swim team.

(left) Just hours after Beckett's birth when Sarah held him for the first time.

All five kids just a week before Sarah's big scare when we almost lost her again.

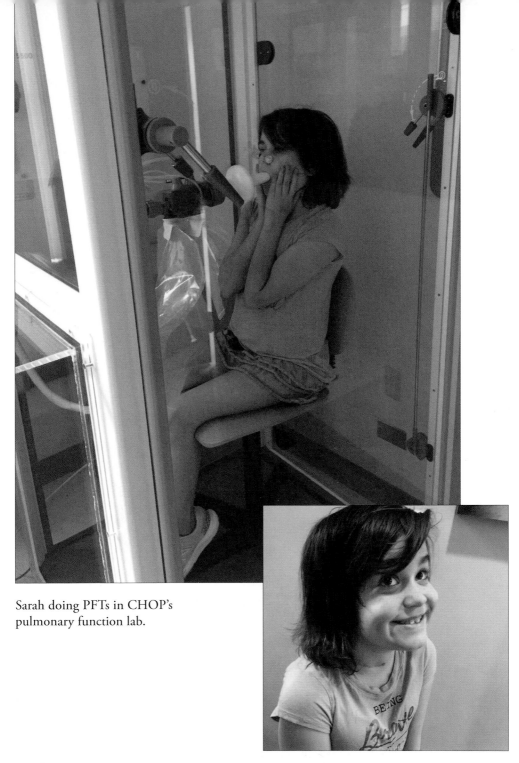

Sarah doing PFTs in CHOP's
pulmonary function lab.

Sweet Sarah four years after her lung
transplant.

(top) Sarah at the beach soon after our move.

(bottom) The cousins at the beach.

obviously proven myself as somebody who is very attentive to Sarah. But I lose the home nursing debate, and later, when I look back, it is hysterical that I was ever delusional enough to believe that I did not need nurses. I will quickly learn how naive I am, because when I get home, I immediately realize I could never have done it without them.

I promise him that the second I feel like I can't take care of her, that I can't do the best by her, that I will come back. I'm the last person who is going to put Sarah at risk or do anything to make this not go well. We start to plan.

As August 27 approaches, we have one last hurdle. We are told Sarah needs another surgery before she goes home. They want her to have a fundoplication, which is a surgery that strengthens the valve between the stomach and esophagus so that she cannot reflux. Most lung transplant patients undergo this procedure, because it is widely believed that the aspiration of stomach contents into the lungs is a leading cause of organ rejection, so it is prudent even for patients who do not have a history of reflux to take this precaution. I am 100 percent on board with anything and everything to protect these lungs, despite hating to have her go through another surgery. This is our last stop in the operating room before homecoming.

# 23. Homecoming

My nerves are high as our homecoming day finally arrives. I keep looking at Sarah and saying to myself, *I can do this. I've got this. Everything is under control.* It reminds me of the *Saturday Night Live* character Stewart Smalley and his daily affirmations, "I'm good enough, I'm smart enough, and doggone it, people like me!"

When your child has cystic fibrosis, you spend a lifetime giving them care. At first there is a big learning curve. You have this sweet precious newborn—or, in my case, a toddler, who needs pancreatic enzymes and "tap-taps" (our word for chest PT when Sarah was little) along with a few other medications. As the years go by, the medications slowly pile on, one on top of the other. New diagnoses are added to the mix, like CF-related diabetes. What may have started as five or six medications is now ten, fifteen, maybe twenty. What started as "tap-taps" now involves multiple machines—and, for us, $O_2$ and BiPAP. But you build up to that. The whole picture looks overwhelming from the outside or if you try to describe it to someone, but to you, it is second nature.

Once your child has a double lung transplant, you take the bulk of cystic fibrosis and trade it for a totally different disease.

Some elements of CF remain, like the diabetes and digestive issues, but the main problem—those sticky, infected lungs—are
gone. In their place are these pink, beautiful new lungs, but don't
be fooled; a double lung transplant is not a cure.

Granted, this new disease is a much better one, but these new
lungs have a whole new set of rules, concerns, and medications.
Unlike the CF lungs that get worse over time, the transplanted
lungs get easier over time. This is good news, but it also means that
when you first go home from the hospital, you are taking your
new disease home in its most fragile and challenging state. The
riskiest times are the first months and the first year. And that's
terrifying.

So, my cocky, overconfident self is having a reality check right
now—that's what the daily affirmations are about. I am coming
to this realization. My child is ventilator dependent due to a paralyzed diaphragm. While she is not on oxygen anymore, the thing
I knew, she is on a vent with a trach, which I'm new to, and she is
entirely dependent on that vent to breathe. Her muscles cannot
do the job yet. Sarah also has a whole new set of medications. The
most worrisome are her pain meds—given incorrectly, they will
have dire consequences. She has new antirejection meds and
other new meds to counter some of the negative effects of the
antirejection meds. She still has the CF-related diabetes, but since
adding nonstop steroids to the mix, her diabetes has become a
whole new ball game, which I am still adjusting to. Add to this
her extreme physical limitations, and you can see why I am starting
to feel intimidated.

On top of this, my child's homecoming is national news. In the
past, it's just been me in front of the cameras. Sarah has only been
on camera in a very limited, controlled way. Further, Sarah does
not understand her fame *at all*. I have been slowly unraveling the
story for her, but she does not grasp the magnitude of it. The
world has been rooting for Sarah, and her homecoming is big

news. Maureen, Tracy, and I brainstorm the most reasonable way to handle the attention. We want to satisfy the media but not overwhelm Sarah—easier said than done.

Tracy and Maureen think we should do a press conference in front of the hospital before she is discharged. This will give us more control and limit it to a public space rather than a personal setting. Unfortunately, Sarah has limited endurance. Just the ride home will be exhausting.

To bring Sarah and all her equipment to the curb on the same day we move home is more than I think she can take, so we settle on scheduling a press conference in front of our home at the end of the day. Sarah will arrive via ambulance in the morning, and around 4:00 P.M., after she has had time to settle in, we will do a go out and talk to the press—and through them—to Sarah's fans and supporters.

"So, Sarah, you understand that when you go home tomorrow there will be a lot of news cameras, right?"

"Sure, I know that. You already told me that," she says casually.

"The thing is, you've become pretty famous because of everything, and so I can't predict what it will be like tomorrow," I say.

"OK," she says, very unconcerned.

"Tonight, that reporter is coming from CNN," I explain.

"Oh yeah, I'm going to get him to play Monopoly with us. It gets boring with the same old people every time," she says.

I chuckle, but I know tomorrow will be a surprise.

Jason Carroll, a national correspondent at CNN, and Chris Welch, the producer who met Sarah way back at the beginning of our public battle, arrive, and sure enough, Sarah dives right in to Monopoly with Jason. He is a good sport, and Sarah seems unfazed by the reporters, so I start to think, *Oh, maybe tomorrow won't be as big of a deal as I think it will be.*

"Do you feel like you're a tough little girl?" Jason asks.

"Yes, very," she responds slowly. She is still strengthening her

vocal cords and the muscles that allow her to breathe. I can tell
it's a struggle for her to speak for long periods of time. She continues, "Because every time I've faced things and I thought they
were going to be hard, and I've done them," she replies.

"What would you like to do when you go home?" asks Jason.

"I would like to play with my brothers and sister," she says. "I'm
not going for easy. I'm just going for possible. And what's in front
of me right now is possible," she adds courageously.

"I really know what a miracle it is," she continues. Sarah's truly
an old soul.

Since Sarah's on a trach and ventilator, CHOP's policy is that
we must go home via ambulance. We are all packed up. It's just
Sarah and me. Fran is at home with the other kids preparing for
her homecoming. It's a big, exciting thing because she has not
been home in 189 days. CHOP does a very good job of privately
getting Sarah into the ambulance in a very discreet way. It is
probably how they always load patients, but it is very private, and
I appreciate that.

When we finally arrive, it's a beautiful sight—home sweet home.
Her brothers, sister, cousins, aunts, uncle, grandparents, and
neighbors are all waiting, cheering her arrival. They have hung
balloons and homemade signs across the garage door and front
door. I can tell Sarah feels like a true princess and someone who
is very loved and missed.

The only news crew there is Fox. Just like CNN, we decided to
give special access to these two stations for allowing us to tell our
story so extensively. Even though it is just one crew—and the lovely
Peter Johnson Jr.—it feels like more once we walk in because of
all the lights and cameras. Additionally, the house is full of nursing staff and CHOP home care.

Sarah is still not completely herself; she is on a lot of pain medication for her back and requires "rescue" pain meds from the
bumpy ride home. She is tired, and the pain medication makes

her groggy at times. But she is more herself than just two months ago. I can tell she is exhausted, and I suggest we do the interview first, as I am not sure how much longer she will last. Sarah puts a "diamond" tiara on her head and the gold medal we awarded her for all her accomplishments around her neck and takes to the interview like a queen. She even breaks out in song at one point, and I couldn't be prouder of this brave, amazing girl.

"What would you say to all the people who tried to help you and believed in you?" Peter asks.

"Thank you!" she says as she pauses. "And just remember this, if you're ever in trouble, and I'm strong, you can be strong, too." I think she leaves us all speechless.

Fran and I are totally spent as Peter and his crew pack up and head out. The only problem is that it's probably only 11:00 A.M. We have a houseful of strangers, plus family, a child with complex medical needs, new nurses with a million questions for us, and a houseful of children who have not had their mom for months. Emotions are soaring up and down, mine included. I tell myself that I just need to make it to that 4:00 P.M. press conference and then I will be good. *I can do this. I've got this. Everything is under control.*

I try my best to rally and be supermom. The kids and I break out a craft at the kitchen table. They are all huddled around; everyone wants a piece of me. What was I thinking? I am quickly pulled aside by a nurse, whose name is Kim, with an immediate concern—narcotics. She wants to make sure she has the schedule down pat. Right away, there is a discrepancy, and we both agree we need to call CHOP. I have been home for two hours, and I am already calling! *I can do this. I've got this. Everything is under control.*

Kim's not the only nurse here, but she is clearly the main nurse who will be part of the team moving forward. I can tell I'm not the only one sweating this. Kim seems stressed, too, and honestly, it is reassuring to me that someone other than Fran and me is worried, too. It's not all down to us.

Handing over responsibility and care of Sarah in our home is harder than at CHOP, where we had an entire hospital to fall back on if something went wrong. I am acutely aware that we are more vulnerable here. So even though we have nurses, I feel like we have to manage it all 24–7, to be on top of it all, until we know that they are on top of it. I cannot blindly trust anyone when it comes to Sarah's care.

These first hours at home are exhausting for me because I am trying to wear too many hats. I am trying to be a mommy who is chipper and happy with my very emotional kids who missed me when I was away. I am trying to support, encourage, and comfort Sarah. And I am trying to be on top of all her medical stuff, which is quite overwhelming.

Plus, in a few short hours, Fran and I will lead a press conference outside our front door. I cautiously go look outside my front window and almost have a heart attack. Dozens and dozens of press vans are lined up in front of my house, cameras all pointing this way. *I can do this. I've got this. Everything is under control.*

It's becoming clear to me that I was out of my mind to think I did not need nursing help. I am barely hanging on *with* nursing support, and we have only been home a few hours.

As we approach our big event at 4:00 P.M. with slight terror at the size of our audience, Sarah's back is killing her. She has moved more today than any day since transplant, and she is now paying the price. She feels defeated.

"I can't walk! I can't do it! You have to carry me!" she cries, trying to swipe her tears away. She is so disappointed to not be able to show off her abilities. We set her on one of our living room chairs on the front porch. None of us is prepared for the crowd amassed outside. Sarah looks shell-shocked, and I feel badly that I did not prepare her adequately for this, but it is way more than even I expected. Sarah rolls with it and waves at the cameras as Fran and I answer questions. We are overwhelmed. We are tired. We are emotionally spent.

As I walk back inside, ready to collapse, I have a sinking feeling. A new nursing shift is about to come on, and my dance of learning to trust will have to start all over again. I wish Kim could just stay. I already like her. I'm exhausted, and I feel like Fran and I need to be in charge all night long. And that's an overwhelming feeling. I start to worry. *Did I make a mistake bringing her home? A feeling of panic rolls over me. I can do this. I've got this. Everything is under control.*

## Sarah

I am so happy to finally be going home. At times, it seemed like this day would never come. It seemed like I would live in the hospital forever, just waiting and waiting for lungs. Sometimes I tried to not even think about home anymore, because it made me so sad and homesick.

Last night, Mom told me that there would be a lot of people there when I got home, like newspeople with cameras and reporters and family, too. I know some reporters have interviewed me before, so I just thought maybe two or three of them would be there. Mostly, I was only imagining my family.

So, when I get home, I am shocked. I thought Mom was exaggerating. It just seemed like such a crazy story when she acted like the world was following my homecoming. How am I supposed to believe that? So, I didn't really worry about it. Now that they are all here, I mostly want them all to leave. I mean, it's nice that everyone cares, but this is too much. I am exhausted, and my back hurts, and there are too many strangers in and outside of my house. I just want to be with my family.

# 24. New Normal

The first two weeks home can only be described as hell. We have twenty-four-hour nursing care, but that means there is little consistency in who is walking through the door, so we are on alert 24–7. It is overwhelming. I do not have a feeling of trust and safety with all the nurses because I don't see them often enough to develop a relationship with them.

It's a relief when, after two weeks, our nursing changes from three shifts a day to two shifts a day. This might seem counterintuitive, but it does two important things for me: I now have a very specific team, and I have eight hours a day alone with just my family. Fran and I make the decision that one of us will always sleep in Sarah's room at night, so a continuation of our together but very separate lives, even though there is a nurse present. We take turns, and just the simple act of Fran and me alternating who sleeps with Sarah means that every other night, for the first time in months, I get a full night of sleep—it is life-changing.

By week three, we are settling in. Our core group of nurses is an important piece of the puzzle; I could never do it without them. Having women in your home helping you love and care for your sick child is such an intimate thing, and they quickly become not just Sarah's nurses but also our dear friends. They are people Sarah and I trust.

For a long time now, I've been living in a sort of alternate universe, either locked in a hospital or confined only to my home because of my child's large oxygen needs. It is hard to just jump back into life. I don't know where to even start. Sarah's nurses become people who help me navigate back into the real world again. It's a big thing for me to start taking Sarah out and about, to start letting down some of the guards I have in place. We have led a very sheltered, isolated existence, and there is a process for me to let some of that go. The nurses are a huge part of that. I would be lost without them.

The new daily grind is hard. We do physical therapy five days a week, four days locally and one day in the city, plus we see the lung transplant team in the city once a week. Our nurse Kim has the hardest day—the day we go into Philadelphia for doctor visits and more aggressive rehab; she gets us at our worst, but you would never know it from her attitude.

Today we have a follow-up with lung transplant. Clinic days are hours long and tiring for a healthy kid, which is not who Sarah is. She lies across the exam table half-awake. Her wonderful team comes in one by one, reviewing everything with Kim and me. One of my biggest concerns is her rapid weight gain combined with the continuation of aggressive G-tube feeds. Do we want her to continue gaining weight like this? Sarah eats almost nothing by mouth because she is not hungry; I think she is being overfed. If they are overfeeding her, how will she ever have a normal appetite? Is all this excessive weight good for her broken back? I am frustrated and feel like the nutritionist is not listening to me; she makes the most minor adjustment to Sarah's feeds, and I feel ignored.

It's been an exhausting day, and Kim and I pack up all of

Sarah's belongings, gently help her back into her wheelchair, and walk toward the exit. Standing at the elevator, I'm just totally spent and cranky, and so is Sarah, but Kim is beaming. Since that first day with the lights, cameras, and stress, Kim's been a constant in our home, and she is always cheerful. Right now, she is chatting me up, full of energy. Sometimes Kim's endless energy is more than I can handle, but most of the time it's a welcome distraction from the drudgery that is our daily grind. She makes me laugh when I feel like crying. Today is no exception.

As the elevator doors open and I push Sarah in, I notice the only other person in the elevator is an unusually tall, attractive man. When I say tall, I mean like over six foot five. It's the kind of tall that's impossible not to notice and makes you think, *Wow, he's tall.* You think that, but you don't say it out loud, right? If you're Kim, you do.

"How tall are *you*?" Kim exclaims in a high-pitched, flirty voice that immediately turns this man's face red with embarrassment.

"Um, six-six," he responds, clearly embarrassed but also flattered.

Without missing a beat, Kim takes her hand and reaches it up to his shoulder and runs it down his arm, exclaiming, "*Oh*, that's what *that* looks like!"

Just then the doors open, and the man practically runs out of the elevator tripping over himself. I struggle to hold in my laughter until the doors close. After that, the two of us are hysterical the rest of the ride home. And while it seems like she was flirting with him, that's not what it's about at all. Kim's medicine is laughter, and she brings it all the time. If this nursing thing doesn't work out for her, she should try stand-up comedy.

Sarah's nurse Shannon is with us most days and quickly becomes someone I consider a close friend. She has three kids, similar in age to mine, and we can relate on so many levels. It's easy to have Shannon around. Shannon's fun, always thinking of things we can do together with Sarah. Every day, Shannon and I pack up all our equipment and rally Sarah, Finn, and Alex (who are home full-time because I decided to skip germy preschool this year) and head off to physical therapy at a local CHOP facility. It's a much easier day than the one with Kim. And Shannon and I get into a good comfortable rhythm doing this day after day, week after week.

This PT is sweet and gentle with Sarah, slowly working on the very basic skills she has lost. Regaining her balance is priority number one because without that, she cannot walk independently. She is also trying to increase Sarah's endurance for things like standing. Little by little, this work starts to pay off; before we started this physical therapy, I could barely get Sarah moving. Now, she's doing circles around the downstairs with her walker.

One day, while walking without her walker during physical therapy, Sarah experiences a terrible pain in her foot and falls into my arms crying. I am alarmed because Sarah is a tough kid with a high pain tolerance, but she has osteoporosis from being bedridden and is on high-dose steroids, and we have seen an orthopedic specialist for her back fractures. Now, we fear she has broken another bone and in an alarmingly easy way. We go home and ice the foot, hoping it is only a minor injury, but the pain does not improve, and we find ourselves back in the orthopedist's office.

While awaiting X-ray results, a woman approaches me and says, "Excuse me, I'm not sure if you remember me or not, but our girls were both in the PICU together."

I recognize her immediately as Julie's mom. Julie is the teen who was in an ATV accident and who coded while we were in the PICU. When we left the PICU for Sarah's first transplant, the family was still there hanging on by a thread. Then I never knew what happened, because a month later when we returned to the PICU, they were gone.

Now, she turns and points behind her to a beautiful, healthy girl who is fully recovered. Julie shyly introduces herself. Sarah and Julie do not understand the significance of this moment as we introduce our daughters. Once upon a time, they were both dying just doors apart from each other. The mom looks at Sarah and I look at Julie, and we both tear up and hug. Both these kids had death sentences, and CHOP saved them both.

Later that day, we learn that Sarah has fractures in both her feet, not just the one she was complaining about. Now she's sporting two hefty black boots, one on each foot, but it will *not* hold us back. Look how far we have come. Look at Sarah and Julie—onward.

As the weeks and months march forward, Sarah is getting more and more physically capable and less and less medicated. The sedated, immobile kid I brought home is slowly being replaced. I decide that I think that Sarah can handle more of Dr. Mike's kind of rehab and less of the gentle PT. After some arm twisting, we convince Dr. Mike to see Sarah twice a week. This means more exhausting days downtown, but we counter that by dropping down to four days of physical therapy a week instead of five. We now have a day for fun!

Kim is still my partner for one of the now two hard days with Dr. Mike, and she has a hysterical way of egging him on and distracting me and Sarah from the actual work Sarah is doing. It is genius, really.

Today, Kim gets Mike to tell her about his life. She is dragging as much personal information from him as possible. He is being a good sport but periodically giving me this look like, *Is she serious?* She has gotten him to complain about his busy schedule between his work life and his home life, and she is listening intently—sympathetically, even—asking detailed follow-up questions.

"Wow, Mike, that sounds hard!" she exclaims as she walks toward him. I am thinking, *What is she doing? Is she going to give him a hug? His story wasn't that sad.*

But she's got her pen in her hand and distinctly removes the cap and walks right up and starts drawing on Dr. Mike's nice scrubs. Drawing on him!

"What are you doing?" he exclaims.

"Ohhh," she says in her high-pitched voice. "I thought you deserved a medal, so I'm giving you one," she says mockingly.

I almost die. I am somewhere between horror and hysterical, and Mike's face—priceless. I am sure that just like me, he will never forget his days with Kim.

Over time, I talk Dr. Mike into three days a week with Sarah, which takes some pushing. He has a busy schedule. Then Shannon and I concoct a plan. I pull Sarah out of all other PT, and we decide to do our own PT with Sarah by taking her out for fun. Most of what is happening at the local location at this point is getting Sarah up and moving. And so, we stop going. They did good by her for a long time, and I appreciate that, but they have gotten her to a point where I can do Sarah's rehab outside the clinical setting.

Shannon's a master at fun. She plans trips to parks, mini-golf, the mall, the list goes on and on. I would never have done quite as good of a job on my own. Some days I feel like it would be hard to get up and out without Shannon. There are moments when the tedious nature of the rehab is depressing, and Shannon in particular keeps me going.

Life is improving all around. We have gone from just surviving to really living. Our days might not be what most people would call fun, but Sarah seems content.

## Sarah

Every day is really, really tiring because of therapy. We have to go to all these different, crazy rehab places, a bunch of days with a bunch of different people. I really don't like it, but I know

I have to do it if I ever want to walk again and move around like I used to. I can't believe how hard all of this is.

Dr. Mike has me doing all sorts of things like the treadmill, weights, balance beams, getting from kneeling to standing. I don't like it, especially the treadmill; I hate the treadmill. The treadmill makes my feet hurt, especially if I do it for too long or if I have to run. I can tell my legs are really, really weak, which is a big part of the problem.

I really like Dr. Mike. He's funny and nice, but I don't appreciate what we are doing here. Even when I need a break and I sit down, Dr. Mike's right there with some weights for me—gee, thanks. It's hard for me to see improvement even though everyone says it's happening. It's not just rehab with Dr. Mike I don't like. I don't like any of it, but his is the hardest. Mom says that's why she likes Dr. Mike the best, because he is the hardest, and I just don't know what to say to that woman when she says that—how rude.

It's fun when Mom and Shannon start taking me to the mall and stuff instead of the other PT. I think it's just as tiring, maybe worse, because sometimes we just get too far from the car and there's only one way to get back. Do you think they do that on purpose? At least I get to go clothes shopping, though. One day, it is Emily's birthday—Emily is Shannon's daughter—and I get to go to Sweet and Sassy with Shannon, Emily, and Mom. It's a great day. We get our nails done, shop, and go out for ice cream. Shannon always has fun ideas.

# 25. Surprising News

◦─◦

It's February now, and life—while exhausting—is in full swing. Our pace is unrelenting, but so is our progress. Sarah still needs a wheelchair for long distances but uses her walker for anything smaller. She can balance and walk stretches without a walker at all.

We are aggressively weaning the ventilator, and as Sarah's body gets stronger, she needs less and less support. Dr. Goldfarb wants aggressive weaning from the vent at this point.

"We should be able to remove the trach by her one-year anniversary," he explains. And this is music to my ears. We have had virtually no setbacks on the weaning plan.

I guess it's not surprising that I am feeling run-down and worn out. But each day, I am more exhausted than the one before it, which makes little sense because I am getting more sleep than ever. Concerned, Fran starts taking all the night shifts in Sarah's room, but still I feel worse. I could fall asleep standing up.

I'm also having a dizziness problem. I periodically bang into furniture and see spots in my vision like I might pass out. It's got-ten to the point where the nurses take notice and become concerned. Something is clearly very wrong with me, and I am terrified to find out what it is. I know I need to go to the doctor, but what if they tell me something terrible, like I have a brain tumor or something? My fears almost stop me from going—as if not finding out will change the outcome. I know that's ridiculous. For a person who spends her life taking her child to the doctor rather diligently, I am actually pretty phobic about the doctor for myself and rarely go.

My doctor listens to my concerns and decides to run a whole battery of tests. He takes me very seriously—blood work, EKG, quite a number of tests. He says that if nothing shows up, we will do further testing. What am I going to do if something is seriously wrong? Sarah needs me. I am petrified.

After a couple of days, the doctor calls with the good news. All my tests look great. The only thing concerning is that I am very anemic, which he says would explain my exhaustion. He prescribes high-dose iron and says we will repeat the blood work in a few weeks. I should start to feel better soon. I am relieved, quickly fill my prescription, and get on with my life.

After about a week, though, I am extremely frustrated because I feel no better. In fact, I think I may feel worse, which makes no sense. Maybe the iron needs more time. Maybe I need a higher dose. I am puzzling over it when I have the epiphany.

As I am walking through the kitchen, I freeze. It happens in a sort of slow motion, the thought process. I realize I have been anemic three times before in my life, but it's been a few years, and for some reason, I just never thought of it until this moment. Those other three times I was pregnant. It hits me like a bolt of lightning.

Without saying a word to anyone, I run to the pharmacy. This would be our fifth kid. Fifth! Did you ever see the comedian Jim Gaffigan? He does a bit on having his fourth kid, and his analogy at the end pretty much sums up my feelings right now.

*I recently became a father. I became a father for the fourth time, not much applause on that part. Really no applause, right, because after the third kid people stop congratulating you. They just treat you like you are Amish. "Four, well that's one way to live your life. Can you build us one of those wooden fireplaces?" Four kids. Four kids! Do you want to know what it's like to have a fourth? Just imagine you're drowning, and then someone hands you a baby.*

I get home with the pregnancy test and as fast as possible quickly slip into the bathroom unnoticed. I swear that stick is positive before I stop peeing. I mean, right, that makes sense, because I've felt terrible for weeks now. How pregnant am I? When did I last have a period? I honestly have *no* idea.

I'm freaking out just a little bit. I mean, it's a great time for an addition (insert sarcasm). How will I add a newborn to this scenario? I have a kid who can't walk, who is on a ventilator. I can't even take care of the kids I already have without nurses in the house. Will our fifth baby have CF? Will I have to watch another baby suffer like Sarah has? I am panicking. I know that this is an enormous blessing, but I am thinking God must be messing with me right now. *A baby?*

As I sit staring at this pink stick in the bathroom, I realize I need to clue Fran in. He's working from his home office today, so I cautiously enter the room.

"Hey there," I say.

"What's up?" he asks.

"Well, uh, I've got some news. It's, uh, a little surprising," I say, not sure how to come out with it.

"Okay, what is it?" he says, concern lacing his voice.

"So, you know how I've been feeling tired and bad lately?" I say, and I can see the concern growing on his face. He thinks he's about to get terrible news.

"So apparently, there's a simple explanation. I'm pregnant," I say—probably with a panic-stricken look on my face.

He pauses to absorb this and then smiles and says, "Oh, wow, that's great news."

*What! Is this the Twilight Zone?*

"Great news? We can barely handle our existing lives. How can you be so calm?" I say, clearly irritated at this response. He should be commiserating with me.

"Well, because it's already done, so we'll just figure it out," he says. How is he so unflappable? I will never understand.

"How will I take care of Sarah and a newborn?" I ask accusingly.

"By the time the baby comes, eight, nine months from now, Sarah will be a completely different kid. And I'll help out more," he says confidently.

He's right. I know he's right. There's no way to project what Sarah will look like eight or nine months from now.

When the obstetrician confirms the pregnancy, she tells me not to lift anything heavy. I almost laugh out loud; that's just ridiculous. I have an eleven-year-old who can't walk confidently yet.

So now I start to worry about the baby, too, and for the first time in years, I realize I need to take care of myself. This new child is counting on me, too; I have this other little person to think of now. Testing soon reveals the baby is a *boy* and that he does not have CF!

Even though I am still scared, I start imagining this sweet, precious baby, and in spite of myself, I am thrilled.

### Fran

Janet is not feeling well, and my usual advice of taking a multivitamin doesn't go over very well. Granted, I've been making my vitamin comment for years now, and she hates it—and she has never followed this advice anyway. Janet takes great care of the kids when they are sick, but when it is herself—not so much.

I suggest she see the doctor. The doctor orders some blood work, and a few days later, he calls with the news that she is iron deficient. No wonder she feels bad. The doctor recommends she start taking an iron supplement, and I assume that will be the end of it. But it isn't. After a week on the iron pill, she comes to talk to me with a serious expression on her face.

Oh boy, I have been here before. Been here more than once. She is still talking. I think I smile and put on my concerned face. Then she goes, "So I took a test." Time stands still for a moment or two. I am fully aware what is about to be said.

Then she says it. "I'm pregnant!"

This is totally out of left field and a big surprise—a really big surprise—but my reaction is positive. It is what it is. Sure, I keep all the *what the this and that* deep in my head. I am all in with the positive. I smile, give her a hug, and exclaim, "That's great!"

Oddly enough, my positive reaction seems to freak Janet out. I do understand. We already have four kids, and one is recovering from transplant. We do have a full plate. But as we talk some more, she starts to get excited, too. We are both concerned about whether the baby will have cystic fibrosis. Cystic fibrosis is a genetic disease handed down by recessive genes. Janet and I are both carriers, and each time we have a child, there is a 25 percent chance the baby will have the disease, a 50 percent chance the baby will be a carrier but have no active disease, and a 25 percent chance the baby will not have active disease or be a carrier. Being a carrier is not a big deal. Janet and I are both carriers, which is how Sarah got CF. Two of our kids are carriers.

In the coming days, baby is tested, and it turns out that he—yes, it's a boy!—does not have CF and is not even a carrier. So now it is time to hang on for the ride and enjoy the journey. I'm excited. We have been through a fair amount of bad stuff recently, and a new baby in the family will be nice.

# 26. Living Again

In February, Sarah is honored with the Shining Star Award at the Wishes & Dreams Gala, a yearly event that raises money for cystic fibrosis research. All Sarah's classmates from the Country Day School of the Sacred Heart come to celebrate with her, as well as family and friends. Dr. Panitch introduces Sarah for the award:

> *I can't tell you how honored I am to be introducing this year's recipient of the Shining Star Award. I first met Sarah Murnaghan when she was about one and a half years old, just after her diagnosis with cystic fibrosis was made. She was in the hospital, and as I was making rounds, I got the distinct sense that I was being interviewed by this little toddler. As luck would have it, I passed my audition, not because I dazzled her with jokes or fancy footwork, or even my bedside manner, but because I was wearing an Elmo tie.*
>
> *Over the next ten years, at every office visit, I not only had to address her parents' questions, but I also had to explain things to Sarah's satisfaction. Our chats, however, usually left Sarah's*

*health issues, with the discussion turning to her pig collection, all the things Sarah was doing at school or at home, or while on vacation, or just the trials and tribulations of being a big sister to Finn and to Sean.*

*A few years ago, Sarah's health began to deteriorate; one hurdle after another arose, which she met with fierce determination. You could almost see her digging in her heels and setting her chin, rather than becoming angry or withdrawn. She and her family figured out how to intensify their battle with CF while still maintaining the focus of Sarah's life on the things so important to her—family and her friends.*

*Over the ensuing years, despite truly herculean efforts, Sarah continued to become sicker, and her disease robbed her of joys in her life. First, she found it more difficult to play with her friends, brothers, and cousins because she became breathless. Undeterred, she would figure out how to play in ways that did not require so much exertion. Next, she became sick enough that she missed lots of school; when worsening illness made special accommodations at school inadequate, she began homeschooling but never complained about her gradual restrictions. Even as her CF continued to limit Sarah's activities, she would excitedly talk about her new sister, Ella, who would soon be coming to live with her. Ultimately, Sarah's health deteriorated to the point where she spent almost ten months in the hospital. She outfitted her room, creating a home away from home, which quickly became a favorite place for nurses, therapists, and doctors to stop and visit . . .*

*When my children were young, one of their favorite books was* Alexander and the Terrible, Horrible, No Good, Very Bad Day. *I'm sure a lot of people in this room have heard of it. In it, Alexander faces one horrible happenstance after another, with experiences as devastating as having to eat lima beans with dinner or getting his lunch bag with no dessert in it. Such things are so terrible that Alexander thinks he just might have to move to*

*Australia. Alexander reminds us of the petty things in our world that can knock us off our game and ruin our day if we let them. But Alexander never had to fight for his next breath or use a machine to help him breathe around the clock, or face a surgical procedure that he knew he might not survive. Our awardee has done all of those things and along the way has managed to show all of us who know her what strength in character, intestinal fortitude, positive outlook, and true grit can do. All while wearing the most psychedelic shoes I've seen since the 1970s.*

*As a physician in an academic medical setting, I am used to my role as a teacher to other medical professionals and to families. Occasionally, though, we are taught special lessons from our patients that profoundly influence how we care for others and how we aspire to conduct ourselves. I am humbled to be one of Sarah's students, and I hope that I can meet my own challenges with the same grace and determination that she demonstrates every day.*

*The Shining Star Award recognizes a person with CF who strives to live life to the fullest and who overcomes the many obstacles that CF presents. I can think of no one more deserving of this award than Sarah Murnaghan. Please join me in congratulating her on receiving this year's Shining Star Award.*

Sarah stands in her glittery dress, sparkling under the lights, with tears in her eyes as she listens to her hero, Dr. Panitch, say these words. When it is her turn, she confidently takes the microphone. What a moment, being recognized by everyone! In a speech she wrote herself, she first thanks all her nurses, doctors, and respiratory therapists and then gives this advice:

*Most of you know my story. There are a few things I would like to share. I have a really strong family—the best in the world. My mom and dad never left my side, my brothers, sister, cousins*

*always cheered me on, aunts, uncle, and grandparents. You
name it, there's no alone time with this bunch. It's because of them
that I knew I wanted to live. And the one thing I needed to fight
is the most powerful weapon—God gave me bravery.*

*The reason I survived two transplants wasn't just me; it was
the bravery in me, and the knowing that my family would never
give up on me. And I know all CF kids—and kids with other
diseases, too—have that bravery in them, too. So my advice,
whatever you are dealing with, young or old, is to be yourself,
look deep inside yourself for that bravery, and the reason to fight.
For me, it was my family. It may not seem to be there at first, but I
promise it's there. And it will take you to the impossible, if you just
believe in yourself.*

The award Sarah gets this night will later be displayed promi-
nently in her room with a framed picture of our family that was
taken just after her speech.

We have come full circle. It is now June 2014, one full year from
transplant, and I finally feel like we have made it. Fran and I no
longer sleep with Sarah. She is not dependent on the ventilator
anymore. She now walks without a walker and no longer needs a
wheelchair for anything. Her back and feet have healed completely,
and the pain medications are gone entirely. She has the rest of
her life in front of her. I am about six months pregnant, and
the kids are excitedly preparing for their new little brother. Life
is sweet!

Sarah and I pack games, movies, and crafts into our bag for
an admission to the Children's Hospital of Philadelphia. Sarah is
excited as we buckle into the car. We've never been excited to be
admitted to the hospital before. Before the trach removal, we are
required to spend a night in the hospital being monitored; the last

thing they want is to remove a trach and then have to surgically replace it again. Everyone must be certain. We will be staying in the PICU because that is protocol for trach removal.

Sarah and I are having fun. Our room is in a quiet area, and the nurses barely need to come into our room. We spend the day doing crafts, and at night, we watch movies and play video games. It is not the forced fun I once created for her but genuine joy. This is it!

It's the most uneventful hospital stay we have ever experienced. Sarah is healthy—easily the healthiest she has ever been in her life. She passes all the testing with flying colors, and on the morning of June 15, 2014, *exactly* one year from her second transplant, the attending physician comes into our room first thing in the morning to remove the tracheostomy. Sarah is still asleep when he arrives, and she responds to him groggily when he tells her what he is about to do. And before we know it—poof—it's gone. It's so fast and uneventful. In two seconds, it is gone.

"Sarah, how do you feel?" I say, excited.

"I feel good, except you're taking a million pictures of me," she says, laughing.

As she gets up for the day, I am following her around the room. I even take her picture while she brushes her teeth. Yeah, I'm a little excited. It feels like the moment we have been waiting for— the big first breath. Of course, before they removed the trach, she had many moments breathing on her own, but there is something symbolic about the trach being gone even if she wasn't using it anymore.

Surprisingly, they do not stitch closed the hole left by the trach; they just place a bandage over it, and we are told to wait. The hole might close immediately or take weeks; it's all up to Sarah's body, and as luck would have it, hers closes immediately. Shannon and I can't believe it closes so quickly, and we use sterile water over the hole to make sure there is no sign of leaking—bubbles. Sure enough, it is totally closed.

For years now, Sarah's not been able to enjoy the pool. At nine, tethered to an oxygen tank, she would only be able to wade in the shallow end as I paced the side of the pool holding her oxygen tank. I can still remember her protective little cousin Sawyer walking by her side, ready to take on anyone with the audacity to splash her. Then there was the summer of the transplants, when we were confined to the hospital. Within days of the trach removal, the world of summer and the pool is finally hers again. And it is even better than it was before the oxygen. There are no sick lungs holding her back anymore, just these beautiful, new pink lungs—a gift we will never be able to properly repay.

We quickly sign Sarah up for swim lessons. Swimming will be a fantastic sport to work those new lungs, and it will be gentle on her bones. At first, we pick a young, cute male instructor, just to get the hang of it, but soon it's serious business. Sarah decides she wants to join the swim team, and she moves up to more serious lessons. It is not enough that she has learned to walk this year; she is going to learn to swim, too.

At home, she's up on her bike riding around the neighborhood, swinging on the swings, and just enjoying her childhood. It's a very dramatic change. I remember listening to the audio of Dr. Goldfarb testifying in court last year and hearing him say that with new lungs, Sarah could do anything her peers could do, even play baseball, and, sure enough, here she is. She doesn't pick baseball; she picks tennis instead, but the dream is a reality. Sarah is a child again, and this is better than her previous childhood.

For a short time after the trach comes out, Sarah continues to rehab with Dr. Mike. We want the whole thing—a child who is completely healthy, without any lasting implications. That's the dream!

It's not all joy, though; we must part with our beloved nurses. They feel like family, and this part is tremendously hard for both Sarah and me. It is bittersweet. In addition to Kim and Shannon, we have grown to love Sarah's night nurse, "special Maria." I can often hear Sarah's sweet voice through the baby monitor talking to Maria late into the night. The sound of Sarah's happy chatter with Maria brings a smile to my face.

They stay on a few days past the trach removal and get to experience the joy with us. We can tell that it is tremendously gratifying for them to be part of a child getting her life back. These women who have spent the last year caring for and loving my child are angels.

Everything is coming to its conclusion.

Ten days after Sarah's trach removal, we are once again standing outside our Pennsylvania home with the bright sun shining down on us as we hold another press conference. OPTN, the government body overseeing the laws surrounding the distribution of lungs, has made what I affectionately call "Sarah's Law" permanent. Children under twelve can now access lungs from donors age twelve and over on a case-by-case basis. The yearlong study was a success, and I am told that all eleven pediatric transplant centers have written a joint letter to the OPTN in support of it.

"I've been waiting a little on bated breath for the decision," I say at the news conference outside my home. "We know a lot of kids who are waiting and little people who are waiting. Just knowing that they will have greater access is a really amazing feeling. It's not an enormous impact that will change adult lung transplant, but it is a significant impact," I say. "Every life counts."

Sarah's one-year anniversary is a very momentous moment; we survived the first year—not just survived but succeeded, and now the law we fought so hard for is a reality. It feels like the culmination of everything. We did it!

Life moves forward without missing a beat. Sarah has become a very well-recognized member of our town just outside Philadelphia and is asked to be the grand marshal of the Fourth of July parade. Thrilled, she sits on the hood of a convertible, tossing candy to the kids along the route, and receives a plaque at the end of the celebration. Everyone makes her feel like a star, and we are so grateful.

We go on our first family vacation in years to Myrtle Beach. Our hotel features giant waterslides and great beach access. Sarah can do it all now. Watching her speed down the slide is pure joy, which I capture on camera.

"Sarah, how was it?" I say as she reaches the bottom of a giant slide.

"Good!" she says. "Now Ella and I are going to the lazy river."

We follow this with a round of mini-golf, and I excitedly send the video evidence of Sarah's childhood in action to Dr. Goldfarb, our hero.

In the fall, after a summer of nonstop swim lessons, Sarah joins a year-round competitive team just like she planned. It is the same team Ella, Sean, and Finn are on; it's amazing to watch her be just one of the kids.

Her siblings Ella and Sean had begrudgingly returned to school in September; Finn had excitedly begun kindergarten. But school is the one thing Sarah's immune system is not quite ready for, so she continues with her homebound education. We start visiting her old school, the Country Day School of the Sacred Heart, and although I know it must be tough to try to fit back in after everything, she does not hesitate to try.

Despite all the triumphs, there are some hardships, too. Sarah's moderate hearing loss, which we detected in the months before transplant, continues. Every three months, testing reveals she has less and less hearing. Both ears now have severe loss, and this is a huge blow. Sarah has lived her whole life in the hearing world, and it's tough to be learning to navigate life with a severe hearing impairment. We had hoped and prayed that when we discontinued the antibiotics, the hearing loss would stop, but it hasn't. It has been more than a year since she was exposed to those drugs, but the loss continues. We fear she will become totally deaf.

Additionally, Sarah's feet have extremely tightened heel cords, which are causing her to walk with her toes pointed outward. We begin serial casting of her feet where she is casted on both feet with the heel in a stretched position. Each week, they remove the cast, stretch the heel more, and put another cast on. This therapy is done over six weeks, and she gains small improvement, but her range of motion will probably never be quite the same. Long walks cause her foot pain and limit her a bit.

On October 28, 2014, just four short months after Sarah's trach removal, Fran and I have the extreme joy of welcoming our fifth child, Beckett Kennedy Murnaghan. The funny thing about all my worries and stress is that Beckett arrives at the perfect time. Sarah is fully recovered, and we are in a new stretch of life. All the things I thought we would be struggling with are no longer here.

It feels like a new start in life, a turning point. Here I am in a hospital room holding this brand-new baby, and I know I've got everything. Sarah, Ella, Sean, and Finn arrive the day he is born to marvel at him. As I sit in the hospital bed, Sarah sits next to me in an armchair holding Beckett as the other three kids crowd around her. Watching them is surreal; by the grace of God, I have everything and so much more.

# 27. Big Scare

Right before Thanksgiving break, one of my three kids comes home from school sick. It's one of those colds where you see it right away as they step off the bus—snotty nose, watery eyes, but just a cold, no fever.

This is not the first cold to come through our house since Sarah's transplant over a year ago. I have a method for handling these situations. If it's just a cold, I put the sick kid in his or her room with a TV, gaming—the works—and I go in and out taking care of them. I actually wear a gown, gloves, and a mask so that I don't accidentally bring the germs back to Sarah; again, I am a little crazy but with good reason. We also use copious amounts of Lysol on just about every surface in the house. If I think it's the flu, the sick kid goes to my sister Sharon's house; we just can't take that risk. This system has worked for us, and Sarah has had a remarkably healthy year.

I immediately segregate the sick child and take all my usual precautions, but the next morning Sarah wakes up snotty. Like wildfire, the whole family is sick within forty-eight hours. Of course, I am panicked. The doctors put Sarah on antibiotics, and we start doing chest physical therapy—an unpleasant flashback to our days with CF lungs.

Thanksgiving comes and goes. One by one, everyone in the house, including newborn Beckett, recovers quickly, except Sarah. She is not better; in fact, she seems worse. I put her to bed early one night, worried. She is so tired, which is always a red flag with Sarah. I hook her up to a pulse oximeter, something we have not used in quite some time, and her numbers look OK, 95–96—not her usual numbers, but totally safe. Reassured, I turn on the baby monitor, another item I no longer needed, and head downstairs to watch some TV before bed.

About an hour later, the pulse ox alarm sounds. It is set to go off when she hits 93 or less. This is not a crisis number, and the alarm often goes off because the sticky, Band-Aid–like sensor has lost contact and needs to be repositioned. I run upstairs, silence the alarm, and try to reposition the pulse oximeter to a different finger. *Maybe that's the problem*, I think. The number improves a little—to 94—and I try to reassure myself that it is not a real change. *Sarah is in a deep sleep, so of course it looks a little worse,* I tell myself.

I go back downstairs, but ten minutes later it alarms again. This time when I go upstairs, Sarah is awake.

"Mom, I feel out of breath," she says. I try replacing the contact again, but now, even though Sarah is awake, I cannot get a number higher than 93. I am now very alarmed, but I try to remain calm with Sarah.

"Sarah, it's probably because you are so congested," I say. "Come downstairs. I'll give you a nebulizer, and we'll do chest physical therapy. I bet you will feel better quickly."

"Okay, Mom, but what if something is really wrong?" she asks, clearly panicked.

"Sarah, a 93 is not dangerous at all. I will call the pulmonary doctor and run it by them just to make sure, but let's not worry too much. OK?"

"You think I need to go to the hospital," she says, alarmed.

"No, I don't, Sarah, but I want the doctors to make that decision, not me," I say.

"If you call, they're going to make us go down. I know it, Mom. I don't want to go to the hospital," she says, very upset. I know she's right; odds are good that when I call, they will err on the side of caution and tell us to come in.

Downstairs, Fran and I are stressed. Fran loads her nebulizer and begins chest PT, while I call the pulmonary fellow on call. As I wait for the call back, I am relieved that Sarah's numbers immediately look better while getting the nebulizer: 93 . . . 94 . . . 95 . . . whew.

The fellow feels uncomfortable making the call alone and says he is going to reach out to the attending lung transplant pulmonologist, Maureen Josephson, DO. We have never met Dr. Josephson, who replaced Dr. Kreindler when he left CHOP recently and went into the private sector, but I have heard great things about her. When the fellow calls back, he says Dr. Josephson is comfortable with us sitting and waiting a little longer at home since her numbers improved with treatment. I am told a steady 93 is not terribly concerning because she is sick, but that continual decline would be concerning. So, we sit, wait, and watch.

Because of our history, I think Sarah and I both always jump to the worst-case scenario, and so while I am reassured by the doctor's words, nothing at this point will calm me down. I plan to sit and watch her all night long.

Sitting by our side, blissfully sleeping, Beckett is unaware of the stress surrounding him. He is a sweet and relatively easy newborn, just five weeks old. He is sleeping right through the racket of Sarah's vest machine, which aggressively shakes her chest wall to loosen secretions in the lungs and make them easier to cough up.

He is in a little snuggly chair that we call his "bear chair," and he's often found pretty much attached to me, as he breastfeeds exclusively and eats every two to three hours at this point. He is still a very tiny and needy newborn. Ella, Sean, and Finn are fast asleep upstairs in bed.

Initially, after treatment is complete, the number is a 95, but slowly, it ticks back down to a 93, so I am concerned, but we are still waiting and watching. They said a steady 93 is OK. They certainly will want to see us first thing in the morning, but this number is not cause to run to the emergency room. Sarah is wide awake on the couch and worried, and we have put on the TV as a distraction, but it is not making a dent in her fear.

Suddenly, the number is 92, then 91, and Sarah is panicking. We call the fellow on call and let him know we are packing up and heading to the ER, but just moments later, while we are still on the phone, the number drops to 89 and then 88, and the rapid decline is alarming. Sarah is panicked; she feels out of breath. We don't have any oxygen in the house these days. So, the fellow says, "Don't panic; she's still safe, but call 911. We don't like the way it's dropping."

Surprisingly, we have never called 911 for Sarah before, ever. With cystic fibrosis, everything happens slowly, so we have always had plenty of warning when we needed to go to the hospital. When we first came home from the hospital on the trach, there was a potential for rapid decline, which is the reason CHOP home care made a virtual hospital within my house, including oxygen and machines. We don't have any of that anymore.

"If she looks stable on $O_2$ in the ambulance, ask if they will transport her all the way to CHOP," the fellow says. "Your local hospital will not be prepared to handle her; she's too complex."

The 911 response is quick. They get her on $O_2$, and almost immediately, her stats move into the high 90s. They call CHOP's ER, which patches in the pulmonary team, and everyone agrees they will take her downtown. With Beckett still breastfeeding, Fran goes with Sarah while I start packing her belongings to head down after them with the baby. Sharon, who lives next door, comes up to hold Beckett while I pull everything together. We plan to wake the other kids right before I go and move them to Sharon's house. *Breathe, Janet, just breathe.*

They get to the hospital very fast, and before I have a chance to leave, Fran calls.

"She looks great. Her pulse ox is 98, 99, and she is having a great time. It's a long overdue reunion, and Sarah's holding court. I think you and Beckett should stay home tonight and come in the morning; having the baby here will just make it harder, and she's totally fine."

I feel complete and total relief. The next morning, I reassure the kids, pack lunches, and send everyone off to school, and then Beckett and I head down to CHOP. I've packed enough things for him and me to both stay the night if necessary, including his "bear chair."

When I arrive, sure enough, Sarah is happy. She is on her beloved 8-South and loves seeing these treasured people. Apparently, during the night, she looked a little worse, and they used a BiPAP machine while she slept. They have decided to do a bronchoscopy this morning to help understand why she is struggling so much. They have taken cultures on her mucus, done blood work, and started broad-spectrum antibiotics. Everything is very under control.

We are not too concerned at this point. The prevailing thought is that she just needs more support and heavy-duty antibiotics to weather this storm. A bronchoscopy is not a big deal to us, either. Sarah has had dozens of them over the years, especially since transplant, and she rolls off happy and chatting everyone up.

After a short wait, the pulmonary doctor who performed the procedure—a physician I don't know—returns and tells us Sarah declined rapidly during the bronchoscopy. They are transferring her to the PICU, and she is intubated and sedated. Everyone looks worried.

This is a very shocking moment. I am struggling to grasp the severity of the situation. We are led to the PICU room as they roll her in, and there she is with an ET down her throat attached to a ventilator.

"When will you take her out of sedation and remove the tube?" I ask, alarmed as the PICU attending enters the room.

"I'm afraid we don't know," he says.

"You mean this isn't just a post-surgery, temporary situation? She needs a vent?" I ask, horrified.

"Yes, I'm afraid so. Sarah is in critical condition. We need to wait and hope that she can fight this infection," he says.

I can't believe this. Everything was fine just a few days ago, and now Sarah looks like she is dying. It's hard to wrap my mind around this as I stand there clutching my newborn baby in my arms. Fran and I realize immediately that we will need help. Beckett needs to be here with us because he is still exclusively breast-fed, but Fran and I need to be free to manage Sarah's care. My sister Lora comes right away.

*How are we back in this place?* I'm pacing the room with the baby, terrified. He is fussier than usual, probably sensing my stress. I cannot believe that this is happening. It's all been so fast. *How did this happen?*

The room they have put us in is vast in a strange way. Toward the front, there is Sarah's bed and all the equipment, but in the back by the window is a large empty area that extends beyond the width of the front of the room so that part of the room is hidden from view. It is ideal for our unique situation, so we put Beckett's things in the back with a rocking chair and his bear chair, and Lora largely takes over his care in the "room within the room."

The attending physician on service is visibly concerned. Sarah is getting worse and worse on this ventilator. It is a critical situation. As the evening moves forward, Sarah takes a terrible turn for the worse. The lead attending physician, a stellar doctor whom I respect and trust, calls me and Fran into the hallway outside Sarah's room to talk. He tells us that he is not comfortable with Sarah's stats and that he wants our permission to switch her to the oscillator if even one of her vital statistics moves at all. He wants to be able to move fast when he feels this is needed.

"It is very serious. I want to prepare you; we might lose her tonight," he says gently.

*She might die tonight! She has a simple head cold or virus. How are we here?*

"She has a weak immune system. There is very little we can do other than support her lungs as much as possible and hope and pray that it's enough," he explains.

Within fifteen minutes of this discussion and our signing the consent to switch her to the oscillator, the lead doctor decides it needs to be done, and his team of a half dozen or more move into our room. They do not leave our room for hours as they work to stabilize Sarah. We stand and watch in horror, just holding her hand. The doctors here are truly amazing, and I know and trust several of the doctors in her room, having had extensive experiences with them in the past. That is the only reassuring thing I have to hold on to—top-notch care. *But will it be enough?*

How could we be back to this place so quickly and so horrendously? Last week, Sarah was running and playing, and now she is clinging to life. I sit by her side, holding her hand as I nurse her sweet little brother. *I thought we were past this.*

### Lora

It is surreal to be back in the PICU. The afternoon passes slowly. We watch and wait. I don't know what we are waiting for, but I don't ask any questions. Asking Janet and Fran questions at a time like this would burden them further. I listen carefully to everything the doctors and nurses say. At one point, when the transplant team comes in, Janet and Fran ask for their thoughts on what we can expect. From their response, I conclude that what is happening inside Sarah is not unusual in transplant patients. They say they have seen situations like this go both ways. Go both ways?

Beckett is very fussy, so I walk with him in the large area at the back of the room. I burp him, sway with him, change his diaper, rock him in his bear chair, pass him back and forth to Janet for feeding, and burp him again. He is clearly unsettled by the change in environment. I bring Beckett over to Sarah several times and lean in so that his face is close to hers. "Beckett is here, Sarah," I say. "He has been here the whole time. He knows you will be OK and that you will be home soon playing with him. He loves you so much."

In the late afternoon and early evening, Sarah's condition begins to deteriorate. We are told her kidneys are beginning to fail. She swells up with fluid. I have never seen anything like it, and it is terrifying. The attending PICU doctor asks to speak to Janet and Fran in the hallway. I stand next to Sarah's bed holding Beckett. I can see them in the hallway deep in discussion, but I can't hear what they are saying.

When they come back in, I learn that the doctor wants to obtain their consent to switch Sarah from the regular ventilator to the oscillating ventilator the next time her condition changes even nominally. Sarah is in very bad shape, and he doesn't want to lose any time when he decides to make the ventilator change. Janet and Fran agree, and less than fifteen minutes later, something in Sarah's condition changes, and they begin the process of transferring her from the regular ventilator to the oscillator.

All kinds of people come in. I stand out of the way in a corner holding Beckett. There are many people standing around Sarah's bed working and talking about the process of switching ventilators. Something about opening the oxygen and then releasing the $CO_2$ . . . suddenly, the whole room becomes quiet. Sarah's level of $CO_2$ is not dropping down as it should at this point in the process. No one makes a sound. They just stand around her bed watching the numbers on a monitor and drawing blood to test the $CO_2$. There is nothing they can do beyond what they have done. The $CO_2$ will either come down in the next few seconds, or Sarah will die.

At this moment, I am extraordinarily aware of every little detail in the room and the feel of Beckett in my arms. I am outwardly very still, calm, and controlled. I am not moving a muscle. But inside, I am freaking out. I think of Jack-Jack, and I know that I am not strong enough to lose another child dear to me. I can't do this again! No! I am telling God that I cannot handle this.

Although I am not able to see the monitors the doctors are watching (and probably wouldn't understand them anyway), I know the danger has passed when the attending physician suddenly blows out a very audible sigh of relief. The medical professionals all begin to talk again.

About ten people stay in the room for about an hour or two after this. Then, we get back to what passes for normalcy in the PICU. I continue to walk Beckett around the back of the room. Slowly, Sarah begins to look much better. Her swelling recedes as quickly as it came on. It is like watching the first half of the day in reverse. We are shell-shocked, but we know she has turned an important corner, that the greatest danger has passed.

Around three in the morning, we are settled into different

parts of the room. Fran is in the front of the room watching Sarah and the monitors. Janet is lying on the sofa trying to rest, and I am sitting on a chair around the corner in the back of the room, holding Beckett, who is finally sleeping.

Suddenly, in the silence, Janet makes an announcement. "We can never go through this ever again. The next time one of the kids is sick, I'm going to send them down to Sharon's house so fast, their little bodies will roll down the hill. And no one is going back to school. All that matters to this family is keeping Sarah alive. Nothing else is as important as that."


Around 4:00 A.M., Lora heads home. I try to rest while nursing Beckett lying down on the bench in the room, but he is struggling to settle down and relax. Finally, I place him in his bear chair for the night and close my eyes. Fran and I are going back to our old routine; he will do the nights, and I will do the days.

Sarah makes it through the night. *Thank God!* And by the next night, they switch her back to the traditional ventilator. Two days after this, they have weaned her settings to the point where she can be woken and extubated. Her recovery is equal to her decline—fast and furious. It is a whiplash I wish on no one, and it forever alters my feelings of safety and security.

As you can imagine, unaware of all that has taken place, Sarah is very upset to wake with the ET down her throat. She is furiously gesturing at us to take it out. The day she wakes, she is well enough to come off the ventilator entirely. The attending physician comes into the room, and Sarah makes it clear to him that she would like to remove the tube herself, so, with his steady hand spotting her, she pulls the ET right out.

Just before Christmas break, Sarah, Beckett, and I come home from the hospital to the other three children, who are anxious and shaken by Sarah going back to the hospital. None of us can live with this fear. We remove all the kids from school. Finn is upset (kindergarten is fun), but Sean (third grade) and Ella (fourth grade) are thrilled. Protecting Sarah is number one right now, and frankly with all that our family has been through, a little togetherness might be just what we need.

# *Epilogue: The Future*

As I walk into the surgical waiting room at CHOP, it is a familiar feeling. Nervous parents line the room tapping their feet, flipping aimlessly through magazines, and obsessively checking the digital screen for news that their child is out of surgery, out of harm's way. I know this feeling all too well.

I approach the desk to check-in. "Sarah Murnaghan," I say to a kind, familiar face. It has been a year since Sarah's last surgery, before that maybe two years.

"How's Sarah doing? I saw her on the list today, and I could not believe she's fourteen!"

"I know! How's that possible?" I say, but inside I am marveling at how this woman can even remember who we are after all this time. "Sarah's doing great. She's getting a cochlear implant today," I say enthusiastically.

"Oh, that's wonderful. Is she getting one or two?" she asks.

"Just one," I reply.

"Well, the surgery should take about three hours," she explains.

Sarah has been struggling with her hearing ever since transplant, and it has finally reached the point where she is isolated and extraordinarily frustrated. We have talked about this surgery for more than a year now, but always as Sarah's choice, not mine. Just three months ago, she made the decision that she was ready, and so here we are. It is hard for Sarah to make the choice to go into the operating room.

Today, aside from the severe hearing loss, Sarah is thriving. She has transformed from a sick little girl who fought with every fiber of her being just to live and breathe into a fierce, determined young woman who is planning her future. There have been bumps along the way, and this is certainly one of them, but mostly, there's been this tremendous gift—the gift of life.

Sarah's younger sister, Ella, is with me today, insisting that she must help take care of her sister. This plan has worried me. What if watching her sister in pain is too upsetting? Ella is just twelve years old but mature way beyond her years. It is important to her to be here. Fran is with our other three kids. Sean is now eleven; Finn is almost nine; and Beckett is two and a half. Ella and I hustle downstairs to grab some food and fill the script the doctor wrote.

As I guide us quickly and expertly through the hospital maze, I remember what inspired me to write this book. In the months and first year following transplant, when we had suddenly become so public, friends asked what I wanted to do next. A book, I thought. The story you see on TV is captured from thirty thousand feet, and I have always wanted to let people walk this road with us in a more personal way, but the time was never right. Initially, I felt too overwhelmed with Sarah's recovery and rebuilding our lives to do anything more than survive. As time passed, we enjoyed our privacy, and a big part of our emotional well-being was predicated on not looking back too much. But after the initial fame faded and we no longer got stopped in public on a regular basis, I was struck by one exception—sick children at CHOP. Sick kids to this day approach Sarah and tell her how much she inspires them. They have inspired us to write this story.

Our story is not unique. Against all odds, we fought for Sarah. But if you walk the halls of CHOP—or any other hospital—you will find parents and loved ones in the trenches fighting every single day. And it's a lonely place to be. More than anything, we want to tell our story for the families who are out there fighting for survival: You are not alone. We see you. And we hope our story will give you hope and make you feel less alone.

I hold back tears as I walk through these halls today where we lived so many highs and lows. Ella helps me fill the doctor's prescription and grab a hot breakfast—eggs, bacon, hash browns, biscuits, and coffee—no reason to pretend I'll be dieting today. Then we make our way back to the waiting room. This is Ella's first time doing this, and I can see that she is anxious, just like her mom.

As always, the minutes tick by slowly. I remark pretty much every fifteen minutes, from about hour two, just how long she's been gone. "She's been in there two hours and fifteen minutes now," I say. Followed up by, "Now it's been two hours and thirty minutes." I'm not sure who I think this is helping. It is like a nervous tic. At the three-hour mark, my head starts whipping around each time the main door opens or closes. Sadly, for my neck, I am sitting with my back to the door.

A short time later, I am told the surgery is complete. Whew! One of the women from the front desk ushers me into a side room to wait for the doctor's update. I leave Ella in the waiting room just in case there is some unexpected news. I shake my leg nervously as I look at the closed door and wait for the doctor. Every time I go into one of these rooms, I flash back to the moments after Sarah's transplants, waiting for Dr. Spray to arrive. Hoping and praying Sarah had survived. Today is a much different scenario.

I am comforted as I wait this time by the knowledge that this surgery is relatively minor compared to what we have been

through in the past. I also have overwhelming faith in Sarah's surgeon, Luv Javia, MD, who is a phenomenal physician.

Dr. Javia arrives quickly and immediately puts my mind at ease.
As expected, the surgery went smoothly. He tested the implant
in the operating room, and everything is in working order. I head
back to Ella with a smile on my face. Sarah is still in the operating room because Dr. Goldfarb has decided to do a bronchoscopy
while she is already under anesthesia. So, even though the wait
continues, my nerves have eased. We have had more bronchoscopy procedures than I can count.

After Dr. Goldfarb comes out with his update, we are brought
back to Sarah's recovery room, and immediately I can tell we are
in trouble. Sarah is waking already, which is a sure sign she is in
pain. Her pain is notoriously hard to manage with narcotics.
Because of her history with pain, she has been overexposed to
these medications and therefore needs higher doses than a typical patient.

"Oh my God, Mom, it feels like someone stabbed me in the
head, stabbed me in the head!"

The nurse quickly pushes additional pain medication into her
IV line, but it does nothing. She is crying hard. "Why did I do
this? Why did you let me do this? This was a bad idea."

More pain medication in the IV. Again, little improvement. I
had hoped that several years of no exposure to narcotics would
have lowered her tolerance to them, but clearly that has not happened. Her resistance to them is holding strong.

The anesthesiologist comes in and switches from morphine to
fentanyl, and she seems to feel a bit better. But the relief is short-
lived, and she needs repeated doses of this pain medication, each
time with only short-term success. Sometime during this process,
our nurse changes. The new nurse is more hesitant after seeing
the number of times Sarah has received extra doses of pain medi-

cation. Although I understand where she is coming from—she doesn't understand our long history with pain medication—I still feel the Mama Bear start to rise up in me. There is nothing worse than seeing your child in pain.

I aggressively push for the doctor to come back in. I can see Ella is getting uncomfortable behind me, but she sits very silently, bravely watching her sister cry in pain. The nurse is still talking as if we are going home today, and I am wondering how she thinks that is possible since we are dependent on IV pain medication—at least for the moment.

I have had many experiences over the years of well-meaning practitioners who, for whatever reason, are so committed to getting a typical result in every situation that they fail to handle the atypical situation well. So, when the nurse leaves to find the doctor, I quietly explain to Ella what I am doing and why I am doing it.

"Ella, Sarah often needs more pain medication because she's had so much exposure to them in the past. The nurse means well, but Sarah's history is bigger than this nurse's experience, and, frankly, I don't want to ask people to do things they're clearly not comfortable doing."

"Okay," she says. I can tell she is studying my response—taking a mental note. I can see on Ella's face that she's uncomfortable partly because I am being pushy.

"Ella, even when it's uncomfortable to second-guess someone, to challenge them, we have to do it—that's our job today, getting Sarah the best care even if it's uncomfortable."

"Got it!" she says confidently, and I believe she really understands.

"I've asked for the anesthesiologist, the doctor you met earlier, to come back, Ella. I've also asked them to call the pain team here. They know Sarah well."

As I explain this to Ella and she studies my responses, it occurs to me that Ella, Sean, Finn, and Beckett might be Sarah's support system someday, and that it is important for me to explain these things to them in enough detail to prepare them to be her medical advocates. I am training Ella to care for her sister, because our every hope and prayer is that Sarah has a long life ahead of her.

It's hard after you have repeatedly watched your child skirt death to not live in that fear—the fear of the unknown. There's no crystal ball here, but Fran and I have made a concerted effort to live in hope and to live in the moment. Someday life may be hard again, but we will cross that bridge when we get to it. In the meantime, we will live it to the fullest and encourage the kids to also.

This moment of suffering after the implant surgery passes, just as the others in the past, and Sarah dives into the daunting task of learning to hear again through this new technology. She's a kid who's never known easy, so she doesn't expect it. This implant feels like the last stop on the road to putting Sarah back together again. Since third grade, she's been homeschooled and has lived an atypical life away from her peers. We've made the best of it, but now she's just a regular kid walking the halls of her new school trying to survive the challenges of being a teenager. To look at her, you would never know all the pain and suffering, all the strength that lies beneath the surface.

Our little family survived, too. All my fears about failing my other children never came true. Fran and I are stronger than ever. Sean's a typical boy who now spends his days challenging and poking his mom rather than his aunt. Finn knows who his parents are, despite my fears he was too detached throughout this journey. And Ella, well, she's no longer trying to be perfect; she's just a typical teenager. Fran and I joke now that we are in the midst of a midlife crisis. On a whim, we decided to move the whole family to the beach and live our vacation, rather than live for vacation. This is a radical move for us. We are enjoying being together again and functioning as one family.

The many moments of pain and suffering have passed. Sarah recovered. It is frightening to look back at those early days and accept how differently her story could have ended. What if, on that fateful day when Sharon told me the statistics, I had chosen the other path? This thought haunts me to this day. But today, we will look forward to the next big adventure, whatever that may be. I am no longer afraid to look ahead to the future with its infinite possibilities, and just enjoy life.

## Sarah

Sitting on 8-South after the cochlear implant surgery, I finally feel like I can relax again. The searing, sharp pain has subsided mostly, but now my gut feels awful. This part I expected. My stomach is always a disaster after anesthesia, especially if I need a lot of pain meds. It's like you solve one problem just to start another. I am all too familiar with this dance.

But tonight, I'm feeling nostalgic as I look around this familiar place, which now feels unfamiliar. The faces have changed over the last few years; many of my favorite nurses are no longer on the floor. Even the doctor is new to me. It's strange because this was once a second home to me—for 189 days. So much has changed, including me.

Bit by bit, I've overcome. It's been hard, very hard, but mostly, I feel whole again. I guess my hearing is one of the few exceptions to that. What started as moderate loss changed to severe loss in both ears, one worse than the other, but both bad. It's really isolating. I guess you get the good with the bad. That's how I think of it. I survived after almost dying, so I guess, basically, this is just a little sacrifice that I had to make. Without the medicine that caused this hearing loss, I would not be living right now.

It's weird, writing this book with Mom, looking back. Some of the memories are fresh and crisp, while others are foggy and faded. When I look at the pictures, videos, and even news stories, I sometimes have trouble believing it's me, if that makes sense. I'll see a video of myself and think that's so sad—terrible, really—but it will feel like I am talking about someone else, not me. It seems like a lifetime ago.

But once upon a time, I nearly died here, and there is virtually no way to go through something like that and not be changed forever. I think my living is a miracle, and that's a pretty big thing to wrap your head around. I mean, I always believed in God and heaven, but not so much in miracles. After what happened to Jack, I thought miracles were completely false; I didn't believe in them at all. If there were such a thing as miracles, then Jack would have lived. But now I believe if there was the tiniest possible way God could have saved Jack, he would have. And for some reason with me, there was the tiniest way.

There are a lot of heroes that brought me to this place where I am a typical kid who goes to school, but the ones I think about the most are my two organ donors. Without them, there is nothing, but because of them, I have everything. I plan to honor their memory by living my life to the fullest each and every day.

# Appendix: Strategies When Listing for a Double Lung Transplant

❧

I've found there are strategies when listing for a double lung transplant that can increase your odds of living long enough to receive one. I learned these things through extensive research and talks with experts after our ordeal with Sarah came to an end.

Let's start with the statistics, which I know can seem grim and daunting. In 2017, there were 308 deaths, or people becoming too sick to transplant—which is essentially the same thing—among all patients awaiting a lifesaving double lung transplant. This number represents approximately 12 percent of people on the lung transplant waiting list. In 2016, there were 339 deaths, or too sick to transplant; approximately 13 percent of all those waiting for a double lung transplant died.

This means that in the United States today, a person dies almost every day while waiting. It's a depressing thought when you're faced with needing this lifesaving gift. There just are not enough organs to go around. But what may be less known and understood is that it is not merely luck that will determine your outcome. There are shocking variations in survival and wait times.

First, get out of your comfort zone. It's tempting to stay put; you have a team that's been treating you to date, they have been giving you good care, they are close to home. None of these factors should be considered at all. You have one, and only one, question to find the answer to: **Can they get the lungs?** Because if they cannot, nothing else matters. You might be thinking, *Don't all doctors and hospitals who perform lung transplants have equal access to organs?* In theory, but the stats tell a confusing story.

Let's look at the numbers, which can easily be found on https://optn.transplant.hrsa.gov. There's a ton of data on this site, and it can be overwhelming, so I'm going to boil this down to the information you are interested in at this point when you are preparing to list. The "waiting list removals," specifically removals due to "death" or "too sick to transplant," compared with national norms.

Up until November 2017, UNOS broke the country into eleven geographic regions. If there was an organ donor in a region, it would be first offered to all candidates in the region, sickest first. If no one accepted the organ, it would then be offered to neighboring regions. The following is a breakdown of the eleven regions for 2017 and 2016 and a comparison of the percentage of patients who "died" or became "too sick to transplant."

| Region | 1 | 2 | 3 | 4 | 5 | 6 | 7 | 8 | 9 | 10 | 11 |
|---------|-----|-----|-----|-----|-----|-----|-----|-----|-----|-----|-----|
| 2017 | 10% | 16% | 13% | 8% | 10% | 18% | 9% | 12% | 27% | 15% | 5% |
| 2016 | 15% | 14% | 13% | 11% | 14% | 9% | 12% | 12% | 21% | 12% | 5% |
| Average | 13% | 15% | 13% | 10% | 12% | 13% | 11% | 12% | 24% | 13% | 5% |

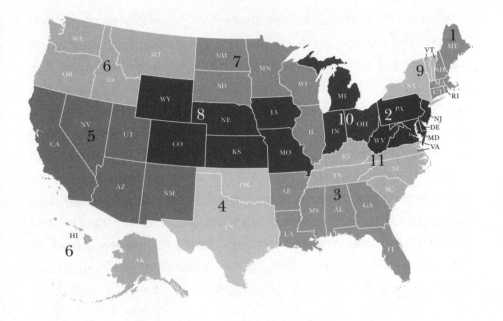

These numbers blew my mind! In region nine, a whopping average of 24 percent do not make it to transplant; that's roughly one out of every four people who list there. Conversely, in region eleven, only 5 percent of patients do not survive until transplant; just one out of twenty die. Then there's a lot of middle ground with lesser but still significant differentials.

In November 2017, a waiting lung transplant patient in New York City, region nine, brought the federal government to court arguing the boundaries providing access to organs were arbitrary and leading to death in region nine. UNOS conceded that the boundaries were arbitrary and not in the spirit of treating the sickest patient first. As a result, they changed the distribution to a 250-mile radius between patient and donor as opposed to specific boundaries. Why 250 miles? Is this another arbitrary number? How about 500 miles or a more countrywide approach as organ viability permits? We know that treating the sickest patient first saves lives.

All the transplant centers in region nine are in New York City, with a massive population, and the transplant demand is fairly low with roughly sixty to seventy people waiting. Are people in New York not donating? I am puzzled. I'm not sure such a limited expansion will truly change things, but time will tell. Regardless, waiting for a lung transplant in region nine, New York, will dramatically increase your chances of dying—so move.

Since UNOS is moving to a 250-mile radius distribution, let's look at the state-by-state data with the same criteria, "death" and "too sick to transplant" for 2017 and 2016. (States not listed do not perform lung transplants. States with an * perform under thirty per year.)

| State | 2017 | 2016 | Average |
|---|---|---|---|
| Alabama* | 30% | 21% | 26% |
| Arizona | 5% | 4% | 5% |
| California | 12% | 18% | 15% |
| Colorado* | 31% | 13% | 22% |
| Florida | 13% | 16% | 15% |
| Illinois | 9% | 16% | 13% |
| Indiana | 2% | 2% | 2% |
| Iowa* | 9% | 0% | 5% |
| Kentucky | 13% | 10% | 12% |
| Louisiana | 3% | 20% | 12% |
| Maryland | 13% | 9% | 11% |
| Massachusetts | 10% | 15% | 13% |
| Michigan | 25% | 14% | 20% |
| Minnesota | 13% | 11% | 12% |
| Missouri | 5% | 13% | 9% |
| Nebraska* | 0% | 13% | 7% |
| New Jersey* | 20% | 12% | 16% |
| New York | 27% | 21% | 24% |

| State | 2017 | 2016 | Average |
|---|---|---|---|
| North Carolina | 2% | 3% | 3% |
| Ohio | 15% | 13% | 14% |
| Oklahoma* | 11% | 14% | 13% |
| Pennsylvania | 17% | 13% | 15% |
| South Carolina* | 0% | 6% | 3% |
| Tennessee* | 4% | 17% | 11% |
| Texas | 8% | 11% | 10% |
| Utah* | 9% | 13% | 11% |
| Virginia | 6% | 8% | 7% |
| Washington | 18% | 9% | 14% |
| Wisconsin | 3% | 5% | 4% |

Did you see that? Once again, we see huge variations with the best at 2–3 percent and the worst at 24–26 percent. Okay, so what's the point? I mean, it's not the state that transplants a patient—it's the center, right? The point is to give you a feel for just how huge the variations are from region to region and state to state, so that ultimately you look hard and close at center data, knowing the variations will be just as huge. It's your specific center's data that matters. What is their two-year average rate of patients "dying" or becoming "too sick to transplant"? If your center does low volume, you will want to look at more than two years of data to get a good picture.

A couple of words of caution. This analysis is very unreliable in pediatrics because the volumes are notoriously small. You will need five to ten years of data to get a somewhat reliable pediatric number. The number should be compared against other pediatric hospitals, not adult centers or overall national data, in my opinion. When patients are sixteen years old, they generally will be accepted at most adult centers even though they are technically still pediatric patients. Lung transplant is very adult medicine, and it's my belief that going to an adult center might be strategically smart at sixteen. The adult centers do the volume and therefore have greater resources in general, so at sixteen you should look at both your pediatric and adult center data. Of course, there are exceptions.

Here's how I would start my research. I'd go to the OPTN website that I listed earlier, https://optn.transplant.hrsa.gov, then go to "data" and then "view data reports." Next, click on "center data" and choose a state. You will be asked for three criteria; first "choose a center," then "choose a category." Here you will pick "waiting list removals." Finally, "choose an organ," which for our purposes will be lung, but this same methodology can apply to other organs as well. Okay, so what now? Let's run the numbers together for a few large sample centers. At this point, I really want to know: 1) how many transplants they performed; 2) how many patients died; and 3) how many patients became too sick to transplant (which ultimately means they died).

Center A:

| Year: | 2017 | 2016 |
| --- | --- | --- |
| Transplants | 59 | 66 |
| Died | 5 | 7 |
| Too Sick | 5 | 7 |

For Center A, in 2017, there were a total of sixty-nine patients, with fifty-nine of them making it to the operating room. We will divide the ten who passed away by the total number of patients, which is sixty-nine to get the average rate of death while waiting—approximately 14 percent. Following the same procedure, the average rate of death in 2016 is approximately 18 percent, making the two-year average for this center 16 percent, which is above the national average of about 13 percent. Additionally, this center has a high number of patients they deem "too sick to transplant"—a red flag in my view, which we will get to later.

Center B:

| Year: | 2017 | 2016 |
|-------|------|------|
| Transplants | 104 | 96 |
| Died | 1 | 3 |
| Too Sick | 1 | 0 |

In 2017, Center B lost approximately 2 percent of patients, followed by a loss of approximately 3 percent the preceding year. They have a very low "too sick to transplant" rate as well. These numbers are well below the national average.

Center C:

| Year: | 2017 | 2016 |
|-------|------|------|
| Transplants | 78 | 77 |
| Died | 4 | 6 |
| Too Sick | 3 | 5 |

In 2017, Center C lost roughly 8 percent of their patients, followed by 13 percent the previous year, making the two-year average roughly 11 percent. This center is performing slightly better than the national average.

Center D:

| Year: | 2017 | 2016 |
|-------|------|------|
| Transplants | 71 | 65 |
| Died | 11 | 5 |
| Too Sick | 14 | 12 |

Center D has a 2017 death rate of approximately 26 percent and a 2016 death rate of about 21 percent, making a two-year average of 24 percent. This is well above the national average of 13 percent, and once again they have a high number of patients they deem "too sick to transplant."

So here are four sample centers with the best losing about 3 percent of patients while waiting and the worst losing about 24 percent. The takeaway is that there is a bell curve to successfully getting patients to transplant, with a handful performing at the very top, a handful performing at the very bottom, and everyone else clustering to varying degrees in the middle.

Why? Several years ago, I spoke at an American Thoracic Society conference and argued there were geographic advantages causing this differential, but after sitting down and listening, I think geography is only part of the puzzle causing the variation; I think if a center employs "best" practices, it may be able to overcome some geographic disadvantages.

Some of these "best" centers told me they are taking organs everyone else turns down and getting as good, if not better, outcomes. Many centers are risk averse, protecting their survival outcome numbers post-transplant at the expense of getting everyone to transplant alive. You do *not* want a risk-averse center when competing for a limited resource. Additionally, some of these "best" centers are traveling to see the donor in person more often, as opposed to turning down an offer on paper only. It's expensive to do this and in general puts smaller centers at a disadvantage. Once you have found a center you think looks good on paper, here are some pertinent questions:

*What percentage of organs offered does your center turn down?*
*What percentage of organs do they go look at personally versus on paper?*
*What is the average wait time for lungs at your center?*

The answers to these questions should paint a telling picture. The shorter the wait time, the better. It's a great indication of how risk averse a center is. One center near me currently boasts a six-day average wait time. This is remarkable.

Let's discuss "too sick to transplant." Why do some centers have many such patients and others have fewer? It goes back to the question: **How risk averse is your center?** I have had several families reach out to me in the final days of their loved one's life and say their center will not transplant now that the person is intubated and sedated or on ECMO. Additionally, now no new center will take them, because the risk to transport is too high. So, here's a few more questions:

> *Do you transplant patients who are intubated and sedated?*
> *Do you transplant patients off ECMO?*
> *What criteria do you use to determine a patient is "too sick to trans-plant"?*

Many people waiting for lung transplant are of a small stature due to the disease process that got them to this point. If you are petite, your odds of getting lungs in time goes down significantly, so you also must know how your center feels about resizing a lung, or lobectomy. If you are a pediatric patient, this is critical information.

> *Do you resize lungs and do lobectomies, and if so, how often?*
> *What are your success rates post-transplant for lobectomies versus tra-ditional transplant?*
> *What are the size parameters you would consider for me?*

The greater the range, the better. We spoke on this topic with several centers when trying to dual list Sarah. I learned that 1) not all centers will perform lobectomies; and 2) many will not do an aggressive size range.

Of course, you also want to hear about their post-transplant outcomes. I believe their first-year numbers are very critical, since the first year is tricky. These are the numbers I believe centers are trying to protect when they are overly cautious on the front end.

*What is your one-year survival rate compared to the national average? What are your long-term survival rates compared to the national average?*

Once you've found a center that looks like a strategic pick, you need a plan B. Dual list—find a second center for a dual listing that is more than 250 miles away and in a different region. You need to do this now while you are relatively healthy, not in an emergency when few centers will be willing to take the risk. I know this is another uncomfortable idea, but it's strategic; relocating will be the least difficult thing you do, I promise. This gives you double the opportunity, which you need. Remember, this is unlike any other medical procedure; you need a limited resource. Be strategic!

My final word of advice is caution. The first year post-transplant is very risky; germs are the enemy. It's hard to be cautious; you've been sick and hidden away waiting for lungs, and now you finally feel well, and the temptation is to not waste time. Your immunosuppression is very high; wait for stable, low-level immunosuppression before exposing yourself to schools, crowds, airplanes, and so on. Proceeding with caution in the beginning will increase your odds of long-term success.

Knowledge is power!

# *Acknowledgments*

To my family: There is no story without you. There is no hope, only darkness. You are my light! Especially to my husband, Fran, for sharing this crazy, messy life with me. It has not always been easy, but there is no one else I would rather walk this road with. I love you!

To my sister Lora, who spent endless hours reviewing this book. You are a world-class editor! Thank you for being a mother figure in my life when I needed one and for always supporting us.

To my sister Sharon, for telling me to fight and making it seem possible. Without this moment, there is nothing else. Thank you for being my kids' mom when I could not be there.

To Claire Tierney, my honorary sister, for coming through for my kids in a big way.

I am eternally grateful to my late mother, Regina Kennedy Ruddock, for instilling in my sisters and me the value of family and for teaching me to stand up for myself. To Sarah's Pa and Mimi, Grandmom and Grandpop, and Nana and Uncle Jim for your endless love, encouragement, and support.

To the fierce, determined women of Team Sarah, who helped change the trajectory of my life: Tracy Simon, Maureen Garrity,

Anne Bongiovanni, Nicole McLane, Rachael Schwartz, Laura Lebaudy, Tracey Santilli, Jill Monahan, and Denise Portner. These friends and public relations professionals tapped every possible media, political, and legal connection. I am forever grateful that they figured out how to harness the power of public sentiment into action.

To the countless others who contributed their time and resources to our family, especially Joe Bongiovanni, Erin Duffy, and the employees of Tierney.

To Steve Harvey, who believed in us when no one else did and used his legal prowess to save our daughter.

To my fellow CF parents, who offered me friendship. I know watching Sarah suffer was especially hard for you. The bottomless cups of coffee in the morning and wine-filled red Solo cups at night kept me going.

To the nurses, respiratory therapists, and child-life specialists on 8-South who played endless games, skipped lunches, and gave me breaks. I will treasure the gift of your caring forever. To our home care nurses, who loved Sarah like she was their own and became treasured, lifelong friends.

To Dr. Mike McBride, for giving Sarah her childhood back by pushing her through rehab even when she fought you like crazy. To Katie Oshrine, our nurse practitioner, who held my hand throughout the transplant process and grieved with me over all our setbacks and "dry runs."

To all the doctors who came together to save Sarah, especially to Dr. Samuel Goldfarb and Dr. James Kreindler. It is because of you that I have been able to watch Sarah grow up from a fragile, sweet little girl into an eye-rolling, sassy teenager. You never gave up on us, even when all hope seemed lost. To Dr. Howard Panitch, for teaching us how to care for our sick baby, answering our endless questions, and caring even when it was no longer your job to do so.

You are all our heroes!